THE TEACHER'S GUIDE TO

SUCCESSFUL JOB TRANSFERS

AND

PROMOTIONS

THE TEACHER'S GUIDE TO

SUCCESSFUL JOB TRANSFERS AND PROMOTIONS

JOANNE C. WACHTER

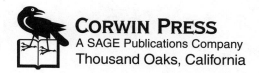

CORWIN PRESS
A SAGE Publications Company
Thousand Oaks, California

For information:

Corwin Press
A Sage Publications Company
2455 Teller Road
Thousand Oaks, California 91320
www.corwinpress.com

Sage Publications Ltd.
1 Oliver's Yard
55 City Road
London EC1Y 1SP
United Kingdom

Sage Publications India Pvt. Ltd.
B-42, Panchsheel Enclave
Post Box 4109
New Delhi 110 017 India

Printed in the United States of America

Library of Congress Cataloging-in-Publication Data

Wachter, Joanne C.
The teacher's guide to successful job transfers and promotions / Joanne C. Wachter.
    p. cm.
Includes index.
ISBN 1-4129-1454-X (cloth) — ISBN 1-4129-1455-8 (pbk.)
  1. Teacher transfer. 2. Teachers—Promotions. I. Title.
LB2833.W33 2005
371.1'0023—dc22   2004027696

This book is printed on acid-free paper.

05 06 07 08 09 10 9 8 7 6 5 4 3 2 1

Acquisitions Editor:	Faye Zucker
Editorial Assistant:	Gem Rabanera
Production Editor:	Laureen A. Shea
Copy Editor:	Marilyn Power Scott
Typesetter:	C&M Digitals (P) Ltd.
Proofreader:	Libby Larson
Indexer:	Nara Wood
Cover Designer:	Rose Storey

Contents

Preface

You have been a successful teacher for a number of years but are ready for a change. After all, you want to keep yourself motivated and fresh. You might be looking for a different school or planning to challenge yourself with a new subject or level. Perhaps you wish to step into the role of administrator or contribute your talents to a specialized field, such as staff development. In any event, you probably feel the need to brush up on your job-seeking skills . . . if you are smart, that is. Even though you already have your foot in the door as an experienced teacher, you will find a lot of competition these days for the jobs within school systems. Do not despair. *The Teacher's Guide to Successful Job Transfers and Promotions* will remind you of all those techniques you used in getting your current job as well as give you some new ideas.

This book leads you through the transfer or promotion process step-by-step. Chapters 1 and 2 help you clearly define your goal and get the big picture of what you need to do to make your dream a reality. Chapters 3 through 5 help you put together the tools you need to make your dream come true. Then Chapters 6 through 10 prepare you for a memorable and successful interview. The final chapter helps you launch into your new job.

Regardless of whether your plan is to continue teaching in another setting or transition to another type of position in education, *The Teacher's Guide to Successful Job Transfers and Promotions* is a valuable resource to help you meet your goals. You might want to read straight through, cover to cover, or sample parts that seem most clearly to fit your current needs. *The Teacher's Guide to Successful Job Transfers and Promotions* will help you move logically, with as little frustration as possible, through the process of finding and getting your dream job. Relax and enjoy the journey as you begin your successful job transition.

ACKNOWLEDGMENTS

Just as I hope this book will help its readers make their professional dreams come true, I would like to acknowledge some people who continually help and encourage me in turning my goals into realities. First of all, I want to thank my husband, Jerry Wachter, for challenging me to make my dream of becoming an educational writer come true and then encouraging me along the sometimes scary path of using my skills in a new way.

I also extend my heartfelt gratitude to two of the best friends and mentors a person could ever have, Bo Ann Bohman and Dori Novak. They have always been there for me through times of both challenge and celebration. They have helped me put my dreams into words and have been my cheerleaders as I turned the words into reality.

Last, I would like to thank Faye Zucker of Corwin and Marilyn Power Scott for their enthusiasm and support. They make the process of writing a book a fun adventure!

Corwin Press acknowledges with gratitude the important contributions of the following manuscript reviewers:

Louise Kursmark
Author, Career Consultant,
   and Certified Professional
   Résumé Writer
Cincinnati, OH

Lisa Burke
Author, Educational
   Consultant
Raleigh, NC

Kathy O'Neill
Director of the Leadership
   Initiative, Southern
   Regional Educational
   Board
Atlanta, GA

Mary Portner
English Teacher
Florence, MA

About the Author

Joanne C. Wachter has been an educator for more than twenty years. Her credentials include a doctorate in curriculum and instruction. She has taught in both public and private elementary schools. She also has had twelve years of experience as a curriculum supervisor. A key part of that role involved interviewing and hiring hundreds of teachers and reading specialists. In addition, she has served on interview committees for principals, assistant principals, supervisors, gifted and talented teachers, media specialists, and other positions in education. Many of the people she has interviewed were successful, experienced educators who wanted to change grade levels, subject areas, or roles. She was often dismayed to see that some teachers, whom she knew were excellent educators, failed to communicate their knowledge and personality in the interview process. She discovered that a little coaching helped these individuals handle interview situations with poise and confidence. In this book, she explains the interviewing tips she shared with teachers who were seeking transfers and promotions.

Wachter is now a full-time writer specializing in textbooks and professional books for teachers. Other Corwin books that she has written or coauthored include *Time Saving Tips for Teachers, You Don't Have to Dread Cafeteria Duty, Sweating the Small Stuff,* and *Classroom Volunteers: Uh-Oh! or Right On!*

CHAPTER ONE

Your Dream Job and Where to Find It

C hanging jobs is not easy. It takes a lot of planning and legwork. As a teacher, you already have a busy schedule. You are going to add to your workload all the tasks involved in making a job transition. Therefore, you want to be sure that every move you make is efficient and effective in taking you closer to your goal.

You may already have your target clearly in focus. Maybe you have taken courses and gotten certified for a particular type of position, such as that of an administrator or reading specialist. In that case, you still need to study carefully the question of *where* you would like to work. Perhaps there is a position available in your current school, and your dream is to stay there. Even if your goal is that specific, you must face the reality that you may not be offered that position. What will be your backup plan? What other locations or positions would interest you? Thinking through these questions is part of making a successful job transition.

On the other hand, you may be itching for a change but love teaching and want to continue working in a classroom. Perhaps teaching another grade or subject area, if your school is departmentalized, sounds interesting to you. Or, continuing to teach your current grade or subject but moving to another school might keep you motivated and growing.

First, it helps to be honest with yourself at this stage. Objectively consider your qualifications, strengths, and preferences. Then, imagine the ideal job that would allow you to use those talents in an enjoyable setting. Consider writing out your idea of a dream job so that you can get your vision clearly in focus. It can take more time and effort to make a transition if you do not do this important reflection first. You can end up trying to fit a round peg in a square hole. The interviewers will sense this and will not see you as the perfect person for the job they are offering. On the other hand, you may be able to say the right things and get the job that you are seeking, but you will not feel as satisfied and happy as you had hoped if the new position does not fit you well. Take this part of your job transition seriously. The time you spend will pay off.

JOB SETTING QUIZ

Whether you have prepared yourself for a specific new role, such as guidance counselor or assistant principal, or wish to put additional sparkle into your life with a new teaching assignment, considering the setting of your job is an important first step. The following quiz will help you think about your options.

Ideal Job Setting Quiz

1. I prefer teaching in the following kind of setting:
   Small town
   Big city
   Suburb

2. I am willing to commute the following distance:
   Fifteen minutes
   Up to an hour
   More than an hour

3. Concerning educational philosophies, I tend to be
   Traditional
   Middle of the road
   Very progressive

4. Concerning curriculum decisions, I prefer
   To be given clear step-by-step directions
   To make as many of my own decisions as possible

5. The kind of principal with whom I prefer to work is one whose administrative style is
   Fatherly or motherly
   Democratic

REFLECTING ON YOUR QUIZ RESPONSES

Now, take time to think more deeply about your responses to the quiz. This reflection will help you define clearly which type of job setting would make you happy and allow you to be successful. Let's consider each item and its implications.

Setting

If you have worked in several job settings, you have probably noticed what a tremendous difference your work environment can make. The comfort, pace, resources, and parent involvement can differ dramatically from one school to another. Be honest with yourself about this. For example, if you are going to be afraid to go to your car every evening after working at a school in the city or fear coming back for evening events, spare yourself the stress and head for the suburbs or a small town. On the other hand, if the idea of everyone in the community knowing your business makes you feel apprehensive rather than secure, stay away from Smalltown, USA.

To research the setting, take weekend drives or walks around neighborhoods where you think you might like to work. See if you feel safe and comfortable. Go into shops and restaurants. Pay attention to what people are discussing. Buy a community newspaper and note what kinds of stories are news items. Ask a sampling of residents what they like and dislike about living in their town or city. Talk to friends who work in different school settings about the pluses and minuses of each type of location.

Be very objective about this research even if you feel fairly familiar with the area. As the old saying goes, "What you see is what you get." If you fall into the trap of disregarding potential problems, you could be setting yourself up for disappointment later on.

Commute

How far are you willing to drive on a daily basis? Some people regard travel time as peaceful "free" time to listen to tapes or gather their thoughts. Others hate every moment on the road. Decide what your realistic outer limit of tolerance for drive time is. Notice how far you can drive before you start to feel impatient and regret "wasting time" on the road.

Also consider what *types* of driving you can tolerate. Some people sail through city traffic jams without batting an eye, while others would rather be called in for an IRS audit than navigate through a metropolitan area. Conversely, driving on country roads relaxes some people, while others feel ready to explode when they find themselves behind a farm tractor moseying down the lane. Take drives to the districts where you are considering applying. If possible, do this during the hours you would normally be commuting. Notice whether the drive makes you feel relaxed or tense. Being an educator is challenging enough; you do not need the commute back and forth to school to cause extra stress if you can help it.

A final issue related to the location of your workplace is whether you think it would be a plus or a minus to live in or near the school district where you work. A longer commute makes it less likely that you will run into Johnny Jones's parents in the grocery store and get tied up for half an hour discussing his math skills. Does that kind of spontaneous encounter sound like an annoyance to you, or would you enjoy being recognized in the community?

Educational Philosophy

There is no one right way to educate children. Some back-to-the-basics programs get wondrous results year after year. On the other hand, there are educators who achieve impressive results by jumping headfirst into the newest educational trends.

You have your own personal philosophy about the best way to educate. Similarly, each individual school has its own philosophy, even though this is tempered by district policy. You will be a lot happier and receive much more support for your dedicated efforts if you are able to match your beliefs with those of the school where you work. Just as a marriage is easier if both people have the same basic values, you will be more likely to be happy and successful if your beliefs match those of the school or schools where you apply. Researching school philosophy is important if you wish to change from one setting to another within the district where you have been working. If you desire to move to an entirely new school district, it is even more crucial to investigate the philosophy of that system as well as how individual schools apply that philosophy.

Table 1.1   Determining a District's or School's Philosophy

More Traditional	*More Progressive*
Heavy emphasis on textbooks and workbooks	Greater use of projects and supplemental materials
Strong focus on standardized tests	More discussion of portfolios, writing conferences, and other means of assessment
Lots of teacher-led discussion and lecture	More group work and student-centered tasks

If you want to find out about the philosophy of a particular district, call the personnel office and ask for a copy of any public relations materials the school system distributes. These booklets, pamphlets, and brochures will highlight the important beliefs of the district. Be aware that you may have to read between the lines to get the message. Similarly, you can request a copy of the school handbook from any school that interests you. Also talk with teachers and parents from that district or school. Find out what they like and dislike about their schools. Notice what they say about key issues. See Table 1.1 for a few suggestions.

The descriptors in Table 1.1 are not foolproof indicators, but they may give you some idea about whether your approach to education would be valued or not.

Curriculum

As you know, educational philosophy is closely related to curriculum. If you want to continue as a teacher but wish to make a transition to another subject or grade, you owe it to yourself to study the curriculum before applying for a position. Confirm that the content excites you. Determine whether the approach fits your beliefs and style.

In addition to the content and philosophy of the curriculum, there is another important consideration: Determine how much decision-making power you will have as a teacher

Table 1.2   Types of Curriculum Guides

Highly Structured and Prescriptive	*Written to Foster Teacher Decision Making*
Uses the word "required"	Uses the words "suggested" and "recommended"
Presents day-by-day lesson plans	Gives general approaches and ideas
Lists required texts and supplemental materials	Suggests a wide range of possible materials
Specifies the number of days for units of study	Gives no time lines for units
Defines a sequence in which skills are to be taught	Promotes the idea of determining the sequence based on student needs

given a district's curriculum for your subject or grade. Honestly assess whether you prefer to have clear, step-by-step directions or whether you are more comfortable with lots of latitude. Approaches can vary greatly from subject to subject even within one district.

Get a copy of the curriculum. Ask a colleague who teaches the grade or subject to let you examine his or hers, or study a copy at the district's staff development or resource center if available. Another alternative is calling the curriculum department of the system's central office and requesting one. A side benefit of undertaking this step is that when you are in an interview situation, the interviewers will be impressed that you already have knowledge of the curriculum. Table 1.2 compares curriculum approaches.

Curriculum philosophy should be considered carefully. If you like being creative and do not like being told what to do, a situation that insists on your adherence to a highly structured and sequenced curriculum will make you feel stifled. Conversely, if you like the security and support of having clearly defined expectations and knowing exactly what to do, a less-structured curriculum will make you feel uncomfortable and not give you a chance to do your best. Be realistic about your needs and match them as closely as possible.

Example From a Structured Curriculum

Unit: Short Story

Lesson: Plot and Theme

Time: 50-minute period

Required Materials:

> Language Usage Activity 37
> Overhead Transparency 10
> Pages 128–142 of *Moving Ahead With Literature*
> Worksheet 21

Objectives:

> The student will
> 1. Define and identify parts of the plot
> 2. Find examples of each element of plot in a story

Procedures:

1. Use Language Usage Activity 37 for a warm-up activity. (10 minutes)
2. Go over the language usage activity. (5 minutes)
3. Put up Transparency 10 and use it to explain plot. Have students take notes. (10 minutes)
4. Have students read pages 128–142 in their literature books. (15 minutes)
5. Ask students to find examples of each element of plot from the story. (10 minutes)
6. Assign students to do Worksheet 21 on plot for homework.

Assessment: Tell students that they will begin tomorrow's class with a short quiz on the notes they took in class.

Critique

You can tell that this curriculum is relatively structured because it is broken down into timed segments. The teacher is told exactly what to do and how long to take with each activity. The specific materials to use are spelled out.

Example From a Less-Structured Curriculum

Short Story Unit

Objectives:
The students will
- Define plot
- Identify elements of plot in a short story

Suggested Teaching Activities:

- Review plot by using plot diagrams. Use a movie that is familiar to students to discuss each element of plot.
- Divide the class into groups. Have each group read a short story from a literature anthology or other source.
- Have each group prepare a plot diagram for its story.
- Provide time for groups to share and compare their diagrams.
- Ask students to diagram the plot of a situation comedy television show for homework.

Assessment: Rotate among groups and listen to their discussions. If any points concerning plot need to be clarified, address them with the group.

Critique

You can tell that this approach is less structured because the unit is dealt with as a whole rather than being broken into time-limited segments. The teacher is given suggestions, but the materials, timing, and the order of instruction are left to the teacher's discretion.

Management Style of Administrators

The building administrator has a strong influence on the school's atmosphere and ultimately on your sense of satisfaction or frustration. Of course, there are effective and ineffective administrators. The reality is that in your career, although you would like to avoid the latter, you are probably going to run into both.

Even among the effective ones, however, there are style differences that you may want to consider. If you seek to simply change your role within your current school, you already know the style of the administrator. You are aware of how this person interacts with teachers. Consider, however, how the administrator works with the person in the role to which you aspire. For example, if you are trying to move into the role of special education teacher, how does the principal make use of that position? Will that approach be fulfilling to you? Will it be consistent with the reason you wish to get into special education?

If you are trying to change the location in which you work, you will also want to determine the management styles of the administrators of the schools you are considering. Try to determine whether a particular administrator is the stereotypic parental type who tends to make all the decisions and policies. The extreme version would be the person who rules "by the book," being very careful that all regulations are spelled out and followed all the time, with no exceptions. This person would suit you if you like to know exactly where you stand and believe that everyone should be treated the same. This type of leadership would attract you if you feel comforted rather than distressed by someone telling you what to do.

At the other extreme are administrators who strive to use a collaborative decision-making process almost all of the time. Those principals generally believe that they should hire good people and then get out of their way until they need help. In this kind of school, the faculty does not have a father or mother figure to turn to for remedies to problems. Rather, concerns are often turned back to individuals or committees. The people who have identified the situation are then challenged to come up with proposed solutions to be presented to the administrator for final approval. If you bristle at being told what to do and feel more at ease when people make decisions on a case-by-case basis, you would do well to see if you could get a job in a school with this kind of administration.

The best way to research leadership styles of specific principals is to talk with people who know these administrators personally. Find out the impressions of others, especially those who work with them. As an alternative or in addition to that approach, pay attention to the administrator's language when you are in the interview situation. Take advantage of the time at the end of the interview when you are asked if you have any questions to make a couple of inquiries that may give you clues concerning how the principal operates the school.

Questions for the Administrator

- What are some of the accomplishments of this school that make you most proud?
- What are the unique features of the school that make it stand out in the district?
- Do you have a school improvement committee? Who is on that committee, and what are some of the things it does?

As you listen to these answers, and later when you reflect on the interview, think about the kind of language you heard from the administrator. Did you hear a lot of "I" and "my" statements or more "we" and "our" comments? Did this person say "I expect" all the time instead of also using the words "suggest" and "recommend"? Also pay attention to your "gut feeling." Is this a person whom you immediately liked or disliked? Can you see yourself enjoying working with him or her? Most likely, you have learned how to work with the administrator in your current school. There is no reason, as the old saying goes, to jump from the frying pan into the fire by seeking a position in a school where you will clash with the administrative style. The principal of your school will be a key factor in your success through suggestions, support, and formal evaluation of your work.

WHERE TO LOOK

Once you have a vision of the ideal situation in mind, how do you find a job that will fulfill that vision? Contacts are your greatest asset in unearthing the position of your dreams. Who you know *does* make a tremendous difference. Of course, you are likely to know what is happening in your current school through your on-the-job contacts. If you are interested in moving out, however, educators in other schools and other school districts are your greatest resource. If you do not know educators in those settings, you may have friends and acquaintances who have children in other schools, and they may be aware of staff openings.

At parties, synagogue or church, family gatherings, your doctor's office, and other places, plan to answer the frequently asked question, "What's new?" by dropping the information that you are excited about looking for a new position. Keep your ears open for leads, and be sure you are putting your best foot forward with people with whom you are talking. You want acquaintances to think about you favorably in relation to any teaching jobs they hear about.

In some cases, the Internet can also be a useful tool when searching for a job. Some school district Web sites have a "Job Listings" section. In addition, check out the sites of professional educational organizations to which you belong. Some of these list employment opportunities.

Another option is to take a deep breath, gather up your courage, and make some phone calls or visits to schools in the districts where you would like to work. A great deal of care and diplomacy must be used in doing this. Chapter 6 will give you some hints about how to make this a positive and helpful experience.

Before you follow any of the foregoing recommendations, you need to consider carefully the issue of professional courtesy. If you are "blabbing" all over the community that you are interested in a new job but have not told your principal, hard feelings may arise. Many teachers who want to transfer to another school fear the step of telling their current employer. Good administrators, however, understand that some teachers keep themselves fresh by taking on new challenges. In spite of being disappointed to hear you are considering leaving your current assignment, your principal will understand. After all, at some point, that person had to deliver the same message to an administrator to become the leader of your school.

FINAL THOUGHTS

As you can see, thinking about the ideal situation for your talents and personality takes time and effort. In working on a large scale, important project such as changing jobs, planning is a key to success. Take this step seriously, and you will experience less frustration than if you jump in without a strategy. You will also be more likely to find a job that will increase your success and satisfaction and help you develop your skills.

CHAPTER TWO

Working the Process

You may think that once you have identified your goal, all that you have to do is tell the right people, and your wishes will come true. This is not likely even if you simply want to change from one school to another within your own district or change grades or roles within your current school. Today's school systems are very careful about equitable treatment of current employees as well as new applicants. Most likely, you will have to go through a multi-step, formal hiring process. This is almost always the case if you wish to change schools or move to a position other than that of classroom teacher.

Usually, a formal application or transfer request must be filed with the personnel department. Someone in that office will check your credentials to be sure that you are certified for the type of position that interests you. A critical stage is the interview with the principal of the school where the opening exists. If you are applying for a different position within your current school, you may be involved in a formal interview situation with your current principal. It is not uncommon for a principal to ask others, such as the assistant principal, a team leader, or another teacher, to participate in interviewing. Also, many systems involve a relevant district-level supervisor, coordinator, or specialist—for instance, the science coordinator or an elementary education supervisor. If you are applying for an assistant principalship or other administrative position, people such as an elementary director and a parent representative may also be involved.

In most systems, the principal makes decisions about who works in his or her school. However, central office staff, such as directors, superintendents, and boards of education may have some involvement in the decision, but it is extremely rare that the principal's decision is overturned. In some systems, both the principal and the subject supervisor must agree on the decision.

Regardless of the district where you would like to work, you will probably undergo at least several stages in the process of getting a job. Most likely, it has been a long time since you have gone through these steps. This chapter will assist you in focusing on your goal and helping you know what to expect.

ISSUES THAT MATTER TO ADMINISTRATORS

Your goal is to succeed in getting the position that most nearly fits the ideal you reflected on while reading Chapter 1. Therefore, the primary task is to convince the decision makers that you have what it takes to do well in the position. This focus should be kept in mind through all phases of the process: filling out your application form or transfer request, preparing your résumé and portfolio, informally contacting school personnel, and interviewing. Typically, school system employers will have the following questions about you.

Administrative Issues

- If you want to change grade levels, can you manage children's behavior at the level you aspire to teach?
- If you want to change subject areas, how have you prepared yourself to be successful in the new subject area?
- If you are changing districts or schools, is your philosophy reasonably consistent with the school's or district's and can you implement the approaches that relate to that philosophy?
- If you are changing roles, what evidence can you offer that you will be able to transfer your teaching skills to that role?
- Will you be able to work well with parents and coworkers in the new setting?

The questions in the foregoing chart provide general ideas about what matters to school principals and district specialists. Looking at each item more closely will give you a clearer idea about the concerns of the people that you will encounter as you seek a new position. This chapter simply lays out the issues. Chapters 3 through 10 will help you prepare to communicate your strengths in these areas through your application, résumé, portfolio, and interview.

Behavior Management

Your ability to manage students' behavior will be of the utmost importance to the school principal and anyone else interviewing you at the school level. As you know, children cannot learn if they are not attending to the instructional task at hand. There is probably nothing more noticeably disturbing to a school's image and climate than a classroom pulsating with children out of control. Therefore, the principal will want to feel comfortable that you can keep students productively engaged using professional, positive means. Administrators want to be convinced that you will be able to handle many of your own problems without sending a parade of children to the office. On the other hand, they also want to know that you have good judgment about getting the office involved in dangerous situations or serious misbehavior.

The people interviewing you will not assume that your past successes in managing a particular level ensure that you will be able to handle children of a different age or different demographics. For instance, if you are a first grade teacher, you must satisfy interviewers that you understand what effective practices might be transferred to fifth grade and what you would need to do differently to meet the needs of older learners. If you are applying for a transfer to a schoolwide position, such as art teacher or assistant principal, you must be able to offer a concrete plan for being successful with learners of all grades.

Subject Area Knowledge

If you wish to transfer to a different discipline within a departmentalized elementary school, the appropriate district supervisor or specialist may scrutinize your application. This person will look for evidence within your application, résumé, portfolio, and interview answers that you know the subject area. As a district-level resource, this person may work with lots of teachers and lots of schools within the system and have very little time to spend with any one individual. The supervisor will not expect you to know everything about the subject area to which you are transferring but will want to see that you have a good base to build on and that, with a reasonable investment of training time, you will be "up and running." The school principal will also want to be assured that you know your field.

Implementing Philosophy and Approaches

The issue of a match between your philosophy and that of the school's or system's was discussed in Chapter 1. First of all, principals and supervisors will want to see from your application or transfer request, résumé, portfolio, and their discussion with you that you know where you stand philosophically. They will also want you to demonstrate that you can discuss your beliefs and the instructional implications of these for the grade, subject, or role to which you aspire. Most systems do not want to hire "wishy-washy" educators who have not thought through their philosophies or who are afraid to declare their beliefs.

Second, principals and supervisors will evaluate whether or not your philosophy is reasonably consistent with their beliefs and approaches. They will be on the lookout for evidence that you can live happily and enthusiastically with their approach to education. Even if you have not had a chance to use the approaches they espouse, they will want to feel confident that you are at least open to learning and using these. If you are applying for a change of position within your current school, you may have a fairly clear understanding of the principal's philosophy, at least in terms of the subject and grade you have been teaching. What do you know about your administrator's expectations in terms of other grades, subjects, or roles, though?

Getting Along With Teaching Colleagues

Although not strictly an instructional issue, a top concern will be whether you will fit in with the other personalities in your department or team and the school at large. As your prior experience has shown you, a school operates like a family. While there are many rewards in being an educator, there are also daily stresses and emergencies. Everyone needs to work together as harmoniously as possible to get through these challenges.

If you wish to transfer to a new school, principals and supervisors will be scrutinizing you to see if they can envision you as a person who will get along with the "rest of the family." Principals and supervisors will also be judging how well they think you will get along with them and other authority figures. Most administrators want someone who shows initiative and conviction but who ultimately knows who is the boss.

If your desire is to stay in your current school, the principal will take into account how well you have gotten along with your team over time. The administrator must also consider how you will affect the dynamics of the team onto which you wish to transfer and how the other teachers may affect you.

If you wish to stay in your current school while transferring into another role, such as reading specialist or assistant principal, you have a special challenge. Your interviewers will be predicting how well they think you can make a transition to relating to colleagues in a new way. All of a sudden, the other teachers may see you as one of "them" as opposed to one of "us." You will need to prepare an explanation of how you plan to make a smooth, effective transition into new relationships with educators who have been your peers.

Interacting With Parents

The definition of a bad day for a school principal is one in which a parent calls to say, "I have a concern about one of your teachers." Problems will arise occasionally, but principals want to depend on teachers and other educators in their buildings to interact in a manner that will not lead to complaints and, ideally, will make parents feel enthusiastic about the school.

To this end, your interviewers will look for evidence that you have the common sense, maturity, diplomacy, and communication skills to deal with parents. Parents have strong feelings about educational goals for their children and can be very emotional about those goals. You have proven yourself to have the ability in your current position to deal with parental issues common to your grade and subject. Things may be different in a new position, however. For instance, if you have taught fourth grade but wish to transfer to first, you will have an opportunity to experience parents' strong beliefs and emotions about beginning reading instruction. Your interviewers need to feel confident that you are aware of the unique parental issues for the grade, subject, or role you are seeking and that you have a constructive, proactive strategy for handling them.

ABOVE AND BEYOND

The concerns discussed so far are the primary issues on principals' and supervisors' minds when they talk with applicants and study their applications or requests for transfer and related materials. You will have to deal with an additional challenge, however, if a school where you are applying has an outstanding reputation or if there is an overabundance of applicants for the teaching position or other role that is your goal.

In those cases, the people looking at your paperwork and listening to your interview discussion may want more than a good reason to believe you can perform proficiently. There may be many people interested in the same job as you are. In those cases, principals may have the luxury of not only looking for an applicant who can do a solid job but also one whom they judge has the "pizzazz" to move their program forward and the diplomacy to do this without making people feel threatened. This extra challenge is not a reason to back off from your top choices of districts and schools where you would like to work but an invitation to let your best self shine forth.

FINAL THOUGHTS

Your basic job in the process of interviewing and applying for the jobs of your choice is to convince the right people that you have the intelligence, enthusiasm, and initiative to quickly transfer your skills to another situation. You need to help decision makers see that you will be able to do this without excessive amounts of training and coaching since time is always at a premium. Your résumé, application or transfer request, portfolio, and interviews are the tools you use to convince people of the many strengths and talents you already possess.

CHAPTER THREE

An A+ Application

Neatness counts! Spelling counts!

Even if you earned straight A's in all of your courses to become certified for a new position, won teaching awards, and have impressive letters of recommendation, neatness and spelling still count on your application or transfer request form. Your paperwork represents you as a professional. Be sure it represents you well. If the position requires an application or lengthy transfer request, your form should be typed, even if you have to pay someone to do so. If you only need to file a short transfer request form, you may elect to handwrite it, but complete the form with the utmost care.

If you are trying to make a move to a school or system that does not know you, your application is usually your first impression. With many forms to wade through, some principals and supervisors quickly reject any application with a misspelling. Furthermore, whether it seems fair or not, the reality is that people question what you think of yourself and how seriously you are taking your job search if your paperwork is messy. Some applications actually have cross outs and illegible writing on them. Submitting a less than perfect application or transfer request form is like showing up for your interview in a sweatshirt. Figures 3.1 and 3.2 show examples of each kind.

Figure 3.1   Example of a Professional-Looking Application

EMPLOYMENT APPLICATION
Board of Education of Baltimore City

Please type or print.

1. Name _____ Browner _____ Lisa _____ Annette _____
Last _____ First _____ Middle

2. Position applying for Elementary Reading Specialist _____

3. Permanent address

40 Church Way _____ Easton _____ MD _____ 00000 _____
Street _____ City _____ State _____ Zip Code

4. Home phone 555-1234 _____ **Business phone** 555-5677 _____

5. Person to contact if you are not available at above numbers

_____ Jan Smith _____ 555-2468 _____ 555-1357 _____
Name _____ Home Phone _____ Business Phone

6. Date of application 4/1/05 _____ **7. Date available** 6/15/05 _____

8. Education

Date of Graduation	Degree	College or University
2005	MS in Reading	University of Maryland
1998	BA in Elementary	University of Delaware

9. Previous employment

Dates of Employment	Position and Location	Reason for Leaving
2000–present	4th grade teacher, Baltimore City Public Schools	Desire to become a reading specialist
1998–2000	1st grade teacher, Baltimore City Public Schools	Wanted experience in upper grade

10. Please include a résumé.

Figure 3.2   Example of an Unprofessional-Looking Application

EMPLOYMENT APPLICATION
Board of Education of Baltimore City

Please type or print.

1. Name Browner Lisa Annette

              Last   First   Middle

2. Position applying for Elem Reading Spec

3. Permanent address

40 Church Way Easton MD 00000

  Street   City   State   Zip Code

4. Home phone 555-1234   **Business phone** 555-5677

5. Person to contact if you are not available at above numbers

Jan Smith 555-2468 555-1357

      Name   Home Phone   Business Phone

6. Date of application 4/1/05   **7. Date available** 6/15/05

8. Education

Date of Graduation	Degree	College or University
2005	MS Reading	U of MD
~~1999~~ 1998	BA Elem	U of Delaware

9. Previous employment

Dates of Employment	Position and Location	Reason for Leaving
2000 – present	4th gr. teacher, Balto City schools	Desire to become reading specialist
1998 – 2000	1st gr. teacher, Balto City Schools	Wanted experience in upper grade

10. Please include a résumé.

The application you may be required to fill out for a new position may be the traditional printed form. However, some school districts are using online applications. In some cases, applicants are required to use this format. In other instances, this format is offered as an option.

Regardless of whether you will be using a paper form or an electronic one, preparing a draft copy is essential. Either make a photocopy of the original application form or print out a copy from your computer before you begin to work. Use the copy as your draft to work on with a pencil or erasable pen until you are sure everything is perfect. Only at that point should you, or someone who has agreed to do the typing for you, transfer the information onto the original form or your computer screen. If you are filing online, don't hit "Send" until you have asked a friend, family member, or colleague to scrutinize it for errors.

FILLING OUT THE APPLICATION FORM

Most school system applications are similar regardless of the district or subject. No doubt, you filled out one of these earlier in your career. At this point, however, you have different types of information to convey. You may also be filling out the form for an entirely new type of position, such as an administrator or specialist. Reviewing each key component will help you to communicate your qualifications effectively and to avoid any pitfalls.

Vital Statistics

Applications usually start out with easy questions, such as your name, address, and similar identifying details. Your primary concern with this section is whether you have made it easy for the school to contact you. Within your own school and system, getting in touch with you during the school year is a simple matter.

On the other hand, a lot of transferring and hiring is done in the summer when you may be on vacation. You would not want to miss a golden opportunity while you are lounging on the beach. Therefore, even if the application or transfer form does not ask for it, neatly insert your cell phone number. Then, be sure you tuck the phone and charger into your luggage and check for messages daily. If you do not have a cell phone, add the phone number of someone, such as a parent or friend, who can be reached if you cannot. Then, be sure you leave your vacation phone number with that person.

Also, if you anticipate a change of name or address over the summer, find a space to neatly indicate this. Put this information on the application itself rather than in a cover letter where it may get lost or be overlooked. If something changes after you file the application, be sure to call the personnel department and ask them to make a note on your application. Better yet, to be certain that it is done, stop by the personnel office if possible and ask to make the change yourself.

Position

The transfer or application form you fill out will have a space to indicate the job for which you are applying. Use the thinking you did in deciding what kind of job would be your ideal. Clearly state any positions that would seriously interest you. Be specific. Chances are you already have a satisfactory job, so do not be afraid to reach for a job that will make your heart sing or a position that at least clearly leads to your dream. Do not write down anything that may lead to an interview that would be a waste of time for you and the interviewer.

Employment Experience

All application forms give you a chance to provide information about past employment. Of course, you have the advantage over new applicants of already having successful teaching experience. You will certainly include this information on your application or transfer request.

Certain other types of job experience may also be included. Remember that you need to convince anyone who considers you for a position that you would be able to transfer your skills to a new subject, grade, or role. You may have employment experiences outside of the classroom that relate to your goal. For example, you may be a third grade teacher who has just been certified to teach music. Perhaps you have taught private music lessons in your home or have coordinated the music program at a summer camp. Include this information to confirm your ability to teach in this area. If you are applying for an administrative job, you might include any experiences you have had that relate to training or managing people.

Pay special attention to any queries on the form about why you left previous positions. Try to be specific so you do not raise disturbing questions. There are many legitimate reasons for leaving a previous position. Here are a few examples:

Seeking full time employment
Grant ran out
Relocated
Spouse's job transfer
Position lost funding

Avoid general, mysterious responses, such as, "For personal reasons." The person reading your application may jump to the conclusion, even if unfounded, that you did not get along with coworkers or your boss or that you were involved in some unsavory activity. Being a little more specific is preferable.

In providing information about why you wish to make a change at this point, focus on honest, positive reasons. For example, you may feel excited about addressing a new subject area or stimulated by the challenge of working with primary concepts in mathematics after seeing how older children make sense of more sophisticated concepts. It may be true that a side benefit of the move would be to allow you to escape from a team leader who drives you nuts, but focusing on the negative rather than the positive is not putting your best foot forward.

Education

On most applications, this section will involve a straight-forward listing of your colleges and degrees. The only task is to check the directions for the order in which they are to be listed and to be sure your dates are accurate.

Other Qualifications or Training

Take advantage of this section on the application to provide explicit information about any extra training you have undertaken. Highlight any workshops or experiences concerning current trends related to the position you are seeking. For example, if you want to teach science in a departmentalized school, including information about attending a hands-on science workshop will show that you are proactive in learning the latest information about the subject area that you wish to teach.

Mention any awards related to teaching or your subject. For instance, being nominated for a teaching award, even if you were not the final recipient, is noteworthy. This type of information shows that you are a serious professional who goes the extra mile as does having your teaching ideas published in a professional journal or being asked to present at a teaching conference.

Also, take advantage of opportunities to fill out sections about hobbies or special skills. Interesting hobbies or ones related to your field, such as amateur archeology if you are interested in teaching social studies, may help you to get a little extra consideration when your application is read.

Extracurricular Activities

Most applications provide space for you to list extracurricular activities. Part of the purpose of this section is simply to show that you are a well-rounded individual who might be able to make special contributions to the school. If your aim is to stay in your current school, this information is probably already known. On the other hand, if you wish to change schools or districts, information about activities such as your producing a play for a community children's theater might spark a special interest in your application.

List of References

The choice of references is an important one. Most applications provide space to list only a few, so make them important. Obviously, you want to list people who will say good things about you, but that is just the tip of the iceberg. The references that have the most credibility with principals and subject area supervisors are people "in authority" who have actually seen you teach. People who work for the school system where you currently teach are ideal if you are trying to relocate to another school or district. If you are trying to change roles within your current school, think about district-level educators who might have knowledge of your work. Someone with whom you worked closely on a committee, for example, might be a good choice.

Of course, before you list people as references, ask for their permission. Not only is this a common courtesy, but it will also alert your contacts to the fact that you are looking for a position. They may be able to pass along information about openings or offer to speak to someone for you. The section in this chapter on "Letters of Reference" and Chapter 4 include additional information about references.

Statement of Philosophy

If you are completing a full application, you will probably encounter a "Statement of Philosophy" section. This portion gives the readers of your application a chance to find out about your beliefs concerning education and also an opportunity to assess your written communication skills. Be sure your philosophy statement is well written. Take some time constructing and revising drafts. Get feedback from someone who will be honest with you.

Usually, application forms provide about a page for your philosophy. There are many ways to approach this task successfully. If you are totally stuck for an idea of how to start, consider using this space to give administrators and supervisors a sense of what you believe about students and teaching. Focus on a few major beliefs that are important to you. Provide several brief but clear indications of what approaches you have used and would use to implement these beliefs. The main goal of this part of your discussion should be to give readers a thumbnail sketch of what techniques are familiar to you so they see that you are someone who can put your teaching philosophy into practical application.

If you are seeking a teaching position, include concrete examples of methods you have used in the past as well as information about how you would adapt these or implement other means to teach effectively the grade or level that you wish to teach. If you are aspiring to a role other than classroom teacher, provide specific ideas about how you would apply your philosophy to the duties of that position.

Also consider including comments that show your understanding of the importance of parent and community involvement in your program. Work in a couple of concrete examples to show how you would do this.

The following samples of statements of philosophy show various ways of approaching this task. The critiques highlight strengths and areas for improvement.

Use this space for a statement of philosophy of education to which you subscribe.

I believe the teacher is a facilitator and guide in the learning process. Teaching is not just covering a subject but engaging students in learning how to learn. Teachers today need to stress responsibility.

Motivation is another key part of teaching. A good teacher must gain a student's interest to be effective in the classroom. Once students are motivated, they can accomplish anything. I think that by equipping students with the skills needed to become independent, well-functioning citizens, we are making the world better for all of us.

This statement of philosophy could be described as being composed of "Mom and apple pie" ideas. That is, few would disagree with them; however, the applicant has been vague. The statement gives no concrete indication of how the applicant plans to put this philosophy into action.

Use this space for a statement of philosophy of education to which you subscribe.

Teaching is an exciting but complicated endeavor. Assessment, classroom management, and instruction must be woven together seamlessly to provide quality education for students.

Assessment

I believe that assessment must be integrated into all aspects of the instructional cycle. That is, I start each unit with assessment in order to determine what students already know and what they need next. Throughout my teaching, I monitor progress with ongoing assessment. Finally, I evaluate at the end of units to determine if students are ready to move on or whether they need reteaching. I believe a wide variety of strategies, such as traditional tests, observation, portfolios, and student self-evaluation make up an effective assessment program.

Classroom Management

Mutual respect is important in motivating student cooperation. Students need to know that their ideas matter. I help students experience a peaceful, positive classroom by involving them in setting guidelines. We talk about what we all need to do so that everyone feels safe and successful. I make a chart of class ideas, which we use to self-evaluate progress in classroom behavior. When students have trouble following the guidelines, I work with them privately to avoid embarrassment. I also get parents involved by sharing the guidelines with them and asking them to reinforce these behaviors.

Instruction

Instruction goes beyond teaching information. It also includes developing thinking skills. I believe students must be actively involved in order to learn. I use lots of hands-on activities, such as writing, research projects, role-playing, and cooperative learning tasks to foster problem solving and creative thinking as students learn content.

Professional Development

In order to do the best job possible for my students, I know I will always continue to be a student myself. For that reason, I regularly enroll in education courses, attend workshops, and read professional books and journals to keep up to date.

This statement is more fully developed and more concrete. It tells beliefs and gives examples of how those beliefs are implemented in the writer's classroom. Using section headings makes the paper more readable and also conveys that the writer is a logical and organized thinker.

COLLEGE TRANSCRIPTS

School systems generally ask you to request transcripts from your college or colleges as you file the application. Handle this task promptly. If you do not, you risk having your application sit in an incomplete file somewhere with no hope of anyone considering it.

Leave nothing to chance even after you request transcripts. Check with the personnel office after a reasonable time has passed to be sure that your transcripts have arrived. If not, contact the college office that handles these matters and see if you can urge them along.

LETTERS OF REFERENCE

Even if letters of reference are not required by the district's procedures, including two or three is a good idea. The people you decided on for the list of references portion of the application are good candidates for letters if they know you well.

If you are applying for a position outside of your current school, call on your building administrator and subject or level supervisor for letters. If these people do not already know you are considering a change, it may take a little courage to ask, but these endorsements are important to your application. Also, if others in authority, such as directors within your system, know your work, request letters from them.

Another possibility is asking for a letter from a teacher who is considered a leader in the school system and who knows your work. This should be someone who is known outside of his or her building and whose opinion administrators respect. Perhaps it seems unfair, but the reality is that principals and supervisors often find a letter by one of their colleagues or someone they know personally more credible than one by a college professor or someone you worked for in a job unrelated to education. Table 3.1 lists some possible candidates to consider.

Choose the references that you believe will speak most strongly for you. Experienced administrators and supervisors easily detect lukewarm endorsements. They can read a lack of enthusiasm between the lines even if the letter writer does not say anything negative.

Table 3.1   Candidates for Letters of Reference

Strong	Less Strong
Current principal of the school where you teach	Another teacher on your team or in your department
Subject area supervisor	Employers from jobs unrelated to education
Principals, supervisors, or other administrators with whom you have worked on major district projects	

Example of a Lukewarm Letter of Reference

Granville Middle School
1214 Macwilliams Boulevard
Granville, Iowa 00000

Ms. Pamela Short
Principal
Washington Middle School
1212 Washington Avenue
Sioux City, Iowa 00000

Dear Ms. Short:

Mark Owens asked me to write a letter of reference for him, and I am glad to do so. I hired Mark as a beginning teacher, and he has been a sixth grade science teacher in our school for two years.

Mr. Owens shows a lot of enthusiasm for teaching. He is growing in his knowledge of science instruction. During his time at Grayson, he has worked on learning to manage labs and other class activities. He makes effective use of our science text and is branching out to use other materials and resources in his units.

The students in Mr. Owens's classes enjoy working with him. He understands the basics of classroom management and continues to work on mastering the fine points of student motivation and engagement.

Mark Owens is excited about teaching and has the potential to become a very good teacher. Please contact me at 555–1212 if you need further information.

Sincerely,
Russell Hammond
Principal, Granville Middle School

Example of an Enthusiastic Letter of Reference

Granville Middle School
1214 Macwilliams Boulevard
Granville, Iowa 00000

Ms. Pamela Short
Principal
Washington Middle School
1212 Washington Avenue
Sioux City, Iowa 00000

Dear Ms. Short:

It is my pleasure to write a letter of reference for Martha Owings. Ms. Owings joined our staff as a first year science teacher and has been with us for two years. From the start, she proved herself to be dedicated to her subject area. She also quickly established an admirable rapport with students.

Ms. Owings carefully plans instruction and labs. She uses not only our district-approved curriculum but also adds her own unique approaches to motivate students. For example, she uses her artistic talent to provide graphics that help students grasp challenging science concepts. She also conducts a study group after school to help students who need more time and individual attention to be successful.

Martha Owings's classroom management skills are impressive. She relates very well to students. She manages to be relaxed with them while keeping them on task.

While I would be very sorry to lose Ms. Owings from our faculty, I applaud her desire to continue her development by applying her skills to a new teaching situation. I recommend her to you without reservation and would be glad to speak with you by phone at 555–1212 if you have any questions.

Sincerely,
Russell Hammond
Principal, Granville Middle School

In some cases, one or more letter of reference may be sent directly from the referring person to the personnel office rather than being part of the application packet you assemble. In these cases, follow through to be sure these attachments to your application actually arrive.

COVER LETTER

If the position to which you aspire requires a full-blown application form, definitely include a cover letter with it. Even if you only have to file a short transfer form, composing a letter to the principal or relevant district office representative to express your interest in the position and outline what makes you especially well qualified is an excellent idea.

Your letter must be customized to your strengths, talent, and personality. Putting sufficient care and time into writing your letter is important because this communication will represent you. While there is no formula you can follow, there are some important aspects to consider.

Your letter should be brief. Ideally, it will fit on one page. Citing a specific reason why you are interested in the particular job for which you are applying is beneficial. This information helps readers of your letter know that you are not simply looking for a random change but that you are also excited about a particular program and believe that you will be able to contribute to it. Administrators and supervisors appreciate sincere compliments about their programs.

Mention any particular "selling points" you have. For instance, if you are applying for a reading specialist position, you should mention a related accomplishment, such as your students earning the highest reading achievement test scores in your school, if that is the case. Briefly point out relevant special recognition you have received or any particular qualifications or training you possess. These may be the same as those you decided on for the "Other Qualifications or Training" section of your application form. Be sure you sound matter-of-fact rather than boastful. You might even pass along (humbly) a compliment you received from a parent or an accomplishment that particularly pleased you.

The following example will show one way to approach an application cover letter. Be aware, however, that letting your own unique professional personality shine through is crucial.

Sample Cover Letter

Dr. Barbara Adams
Lake County Elementary School
55 South Lake Boulevard
Pittsburgh, Pennsylvania 00000

Dear Dr. Adams:

I am applying for the open fifth grade teaching position in your school's mathematics department. I became interested in transferring to your school after attending a workshop called "Practical Math with Pizzazz" presented by two of your teachers. The philosophies and activities they described are similar to the kinds of things I have found to be successful in my fifth grade classes. In fact, I was recently asked to present some of my ideas to all the elementary math teachers in my district. In addition, I have had some of my teaching ideas published in *Elementary Math*.

As my résumé shows, I have taught all fifth grade subject areas for five years. I have found that my favorite discipline is mathematics, however, and I am eager to transfer into a departmentalized school, such as yours.

I would appreciate the chance to discuss my qualifications with you and learn more about your school. You may reach me at 555–1212. I look forward to hearing from you soon.

Sincerely,
Teresa Myers

One of the most important things you can do is take as much time as you think you should to revise and edit your letter . . . and then take some more time. Be sure that there are absolutely NO ERRORS in your letter and no awkward sentences. Ask someone who is exceptionally good with editing to read and correct your letter. Last, think about how you can make your letter look professional so it will communicate the pride you put into what you do. Invest in a box of high-quality 8½ by 11 stationery. Choose a professional, neutral color such as cream or gray. You may be thinking that most people do not use this level of care when preparing documentation for a transfer request. Precisely! Since most people do not go to the trouble to present a professional package, yours will stand out in the crowd.

FINAL THOUGHTS

Remember that your application or transfer request and accompanying materials are important parts of your image as a professional educator. They should affirm that you are worthy of the position for which you are applying. Take your time with this step of the process. Do not send off your materials without letting the most exacting, detail-oriented person you know look through them.

CHAPTER FOUR

A Résumé to Remember

The mandatory application or transfer forms discussed in Chapter 3 start the ball rolling, but they are not sufficient for giving administrators and supervisors a detailed, well-rounded picture of who you are and what you can do. Many districts ask that a résumé be filed with the application materials. Even if not required, preparing this document is a good idea. Throughout your career, you should have a résumé on your computer and continually update it to highlight important training and experiences in your professional development. If you have not started one yet, now is the time. If you already have one on your computer, use this section to help you assess the effectiveness of its key parts.

RÉSUMÉ FORMAT

As with cover letters, résumés cannot be written using a formula. Experienced teachers may use either a standard résumé format or a variation. The variation may be especially appropriate if you are applying for a job different from ones that you

(Text continues on p. 44)

JOAN STONE

5466 Stone Place
Columbia, Maryland 00000
555–1212

PROFILE

- Elementary teacher with ten years of experience
- Strong background in all elementary subjects
- Experienced in curriculum writing, staff development, and integrated instruction

EXPERIENCE

2003–present   Reading tutor for the Reading Center of Loyola College

- Tutored primary-aged students
- Developed needs assessment
- Coordinated parent involvement activities

1998–present   Teacher with Maryland County Public School District

North Elementary
- Taught Grades 1, 4, and 5
- Created integrated language arts and content area units
- Students scored in 80th percentile on national reading assessment

1995–1998   Teacher with Richmond Public School System

Allen T. Wood Elementary
- Taught Grade 2
- Initiated school newsletter
- Established school drama club

EDUCATION

MEd Loyola College, Reading, 2003

BS   University of Maryland, Elementary Education, 1995

PUBLICATIONS

Literature is Fun (Educational Materials, Inc., 2001)—packets for upper elementary reading instruction

"Five Keys to Effective Reading Incentive Programs," *Classroom Ideas*, 12/00—journal article

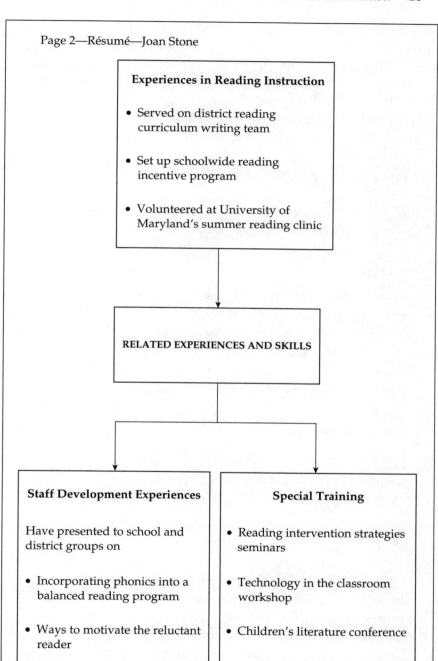

Page 2—Résumé—Joan Stone

Experiences in Reading Instruction

- Served on district reading curriculum writing team

- Set up schoolwide reading incentive program

- Volunteered at University of Maryland's summer reading clinic

RELATED EXPERIENCES AND SKILLS

Staff Development Experiences

Have presented to school and district groups on

- Incorporating phonics into a balanced reading program

- Ways to motivate the reluctant reader

Special Training

- Reading intervention strategies seminars

- Technology in the classroom workshop

- Children's literature conference

have had in the past. For instance, you may be an elementary teacher applying to become a reading specialist or a mathematics teacher applying to become a technology resource person. A skills-oriented component in your résumé provides a way to show how your previous experience connects with what you would be expected to do in the new position. Pages 42 and 43 give an example of a clear and explicit résumé.

CONTENTS TO INCLUDE

Regardless of the format you use, limit the length of your résumé to two pages. There are several parts that should be included.

Job Objective

Go back to the position description you wrote for your application or transfer request. Use this information as your basis. Be matter of fact rather than flowery.

Examples of Job Objective Statements

Too Flowery and Vague: To effectively and enthusiastically utilize my knowledge and philosophies

Clear: To secure a position as a reading specialist

Education

List your college information. Include college, degree, and dates. Also include a subsection listing and briefly describing other training. Note special courses, seminars, or professional workshops on topics that relate to the position you are seeking. In addition, let your résumé readers know about any training you have had in communication skills, such as writing or computer use.

Experience

You might not have much space on the application or transfer request form to describe previous positions held; you can go into more detail on your résumé. Think of ways to make the most of what you have. List the employment experiences you included on the application. Consider adding specifics that connect what you have done with what you wish to do. For instance, being a student teacher mentor could be highlighted if you wish to achieve a position in staff development. Add a few details about special projects and programs that have been your specialty. Keep these brief, but say enough to make your interviewer want to find out more.

Potential employers will want to know what positions you have held, and they will also want to see evidence of your success in those roles. In today's data-driven environment, it is important to include any statistics you may have about your classes' successes on national or state assessments.

The résumé also gives you a chance to elaborate on paid jobs outside of the school setting or volunteer work that may provide additional evidence of your readiness to move from one position to another. For instance, maybe you have done freelance writing for a textbook company. The skills involved in this kind of endeavor should impress someone who is looking at your application for a role such as that of curriculum specialist.

Professional Organizations

List any professional organizations to which you belong. If you do not currently belong to any, join some immediately. Membership is interpreted as a sign that you are a serious professional who wants to stay current and involved in your field. Joining a professional organization or two gives you extra credentials for your résumé. If you are actively involved, you have a chance to network and make connections with people who may know about job openings and also act as references for you. Most important, belonging to a professional organization gives you a ready source of information that will help you succeed in your new position.

Other Information to Include

Highlight any relevant information about awards, recognition, or special skills. Also include a list of references. You do not have to limit yourself to just two or three, as you did on the application, but can include several. Follow the guidelines discussed in Chapter 3 about whom to select. As stated there, letting these people know you will be listing them is the courteous thing to do.

What Not to Include

Since space is precious when you are limiting yourself to two pages, avoid extraneous information. For instance, you can leave out personal information about marital status or hobbies unrelated to the position you are seeking.

ATTRACTING ATTENTION

You want your résumé to be your unique statement . . . to stand out from the crowd. Be sure the attention you get, however, is because your résumé looks unusually professional, not because it is offbeat. If your résumé appears overdone, a potential employer might wonder if you are trying to use a flashy presentation to distract the reader from noticing that your background is not all it should be.

Prepare the résumé or have someone else prepare it on a computer. Choose fonts carefully. Use one that is clear, clean, and easy to read.

Avoid fancy fonts.

Choose a clean, clear font.

Pay attention to the layout of your résumé. With today's word processing and desktop publishing capabilities, you can create eye-catching layouts for your résumé without professional help. A simple border or line, for example, may make your résumé noticeable and communicate that you do things with finesse. To help you start thinking about the possibilities, look at the examples in Figure 4.1.

Also check out computer software that may help you prepare a résumé that is impressive and professional looking while not taking up hours of your precious and limited time.

Figure 4.1   Résumé Headings

Sample 1:

Lucille J. Carter
---

4 Milltown Road   Baltimore, Maryland 00000   555-1212

Sample 2:

JOSEPH GARRY
88 West Church Lane
Olney, Massachusetts 00000
555-1212

Last, choose a high-quality paper for your résumé. The stationery you selected for your application cover letter can be used. Remember that this paper should be classy, not cute. The color should be neutral and professional, not a hue such as bright yellow or hot pink that may be seen as shocking or frivolous. Nor would cartoon bookworms or teddy bears with mortarboards dancing across the page convey the appropriate message.

FINAL THOUGHTS

Your résumé is a tool that you will use throughout your professional career. This document is your calling card giving people impressions about your self-image and the pride you take in details. The time you spend in thinking about its content and design will both help you with your immediate job goal and save you time in the future. As you accumulate more qualifications and experiences, this information can simply be added to the résumé so you will always have a current document whenever an opportunity arises.

CHAPTER FIVE

Power Portfolio

Portfolios have become important tools in job interviews. To make the best use of this resource, you need to make careful decisions about how to compile and use it.

WHAT TO INCLUDE

When you consider the contents of your portfolio, keep in mind that most interviewers will not read the information in detail. You need to create a document that provides at-a-glance information about what you have done and what you can do.

Teaching Portfolio	
Leslie Evans	
Table of Contents	
Section	**Page**
Résumé	2
Sample Lesson Plan	4

(Continued)

(Continued)

Résumé

Most people include their résumés near the front of their portfolios. Including this document is probably redundant, since the interviewer most likely has seen it. It makes sense to include it as an overview, however.

Sample Lessons

Sample lessons are an excellent inclusion in your portfolio. Keep in mind the need to provide information that can be grasped in a quick look through. Even if it means retyping, include bold headings so the interviewer can locate parts of your lessons easily. Use highlighting or underlining to make important parts stand out. Include examples of any eye-catching handouts you used in implementing the lesson.

If the purpose of your portfolio is to help you transfer to a teaching job at another grade or in a different subject area, you may also want to include a hypothetical lesson plan. Create a plan that shows how you propose to teach in the new situation.

Including one or two lesson plans in your portfolio makes sense even if you are attempting to move out of classroom teaching. Your lesson plans are artifacts of the good job you have done in the past. They provide evidence of your educational philosophy and your creativity.

Proposed Long-Range Plan

To further impress your interviewers, include graphic displays of how you propose to handle long-range planning. Keep your wording in the portfolio and in discussing your long-range plan ideas during your interview open so that you do not risk stepping on anyone's toes. You want to show that you understand the importance of long-range planning and are ready to begin immediately while being respectful of procedures already in place. Use the words *proposed, possible, draft,* and *options.* Emphasize that these are ideas you might consider if the school does not have something else in place they want you to use.

For example, you might want to outline a unit plan if your research has led you to believe that there is flexibility in the curriculum. In combination with the lesson plans you have included in your portfolio, a proposed long-range plan will show that you can envision the big picture as well as tackling the details of day-to-day instruction.

If you are aspiring to a position outside of the classroom, a proposed long-range teaching plan will not be meaningful. You may, however, sketch out a proposal concerning some of the services you could offer in the new position. For example, if you hope to secure a staff development job, you might lay out potential topics on which you could provide training. Again, remember that you will be presenting these ideas simply as examples of the kind of planning you might do. Convey that you are eager to incorporate the administrator's ideas about what you are to do and how you should do it into your planning.

Long-Range Plan for Language Arts Class

September to mid-October
Short story writing
Examples from literature text
Mini-lessons to prepare for state multiple-choice reading test (10/18)

Mid-October to holiday
Reading nonfiction
Major research project
Mini-lessons on grammar, usage

January
Poetry unit
Reading various poets
Writing poetry for school anthology
Mini-lessons on figurative language

February to mid-March
Integrated unit with social studies, art, and music teachers

Mini-lessons on word derivations

Mid-March to April
Readers' and Writers' Workshop
Mini-lessons on various genres

Early to mid-May
Persuasive writing
Reading examples: essays, letters, junk mail, political materials
Mini-lessons on grammar, usage

Mid-May to end
Preparation for "Showcase of Writing Talent"
Reading and critiquing to decide what to include
Polishing works to be showcased
Mini-lessons on presentation and listening skills

Productive Behavior Management Plan

Administrators always want to be assured that you can handle classroom management issues in a positive, effective way. Including evidence of your skill in this area is a plus. A concrete plan for managing behavior will be very impressive and comforting to your interviewer, particularly if you desire to change grade levels. Your plan should provide proof that you know the unique characteristics and needs of students at the grade level you wish to teach and that you have specific ideas for meeting their needs (see Figure 5.1 for an example).

If you are applying for a position other than classroom teacher, you may need to provide a different kind of graphic. For example, if you are trying to become a subject area specialist who will deal with all grades, you might want to chart out the kind of positive behavior support system you plan to institute for primary versus intermediate grades. If you are applying for an assistant principal position, a management flowchart might focus on the steps you would use when presented with a child who is sent to the office in need of coaching on productive and appropriate behavior.

Classroom Layout Plan

You might also show a proposal for laying out the areas in your classroom. Of course, these thoughts will have to be very rough ideas unless you are in the unusual situation of knowing what your classroom would actually look like. There are simple computer programs that do floor plans or you could neatly sketch out a room using graph paper and a ruler (see Figure 5.2).

Supplemental Materials List

Depending on your subject area and the flexibility of the curriculum, you might list proposed supplemental materials that could be part of your program. For instance, identifying children's or young adults' magazines and appropriate Internet sites that support your subject area would be proof of your knowledge of your subject area and also attest to your initiative and resourcefulness.

Figure 5.1   Behavior Management Plan

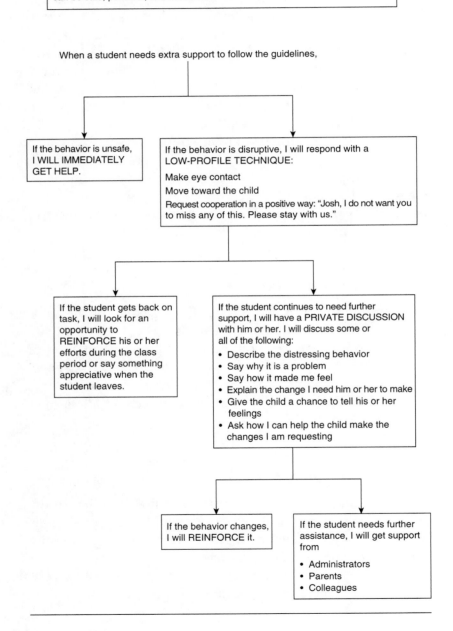

Figure 5.2   Sample Classroom Layout

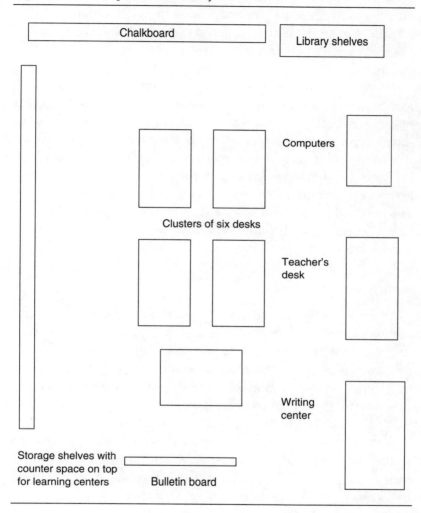

Photographs

Photos are good additions to your portfolio since they convey information about the kinds of things you have done in your classroom. They also convey something about the instructional tone you set. You will need to plan ahead to get several classroom photos if you do not already have a collection. Take photographs of students at work. Show special areas of your room, such as a comfortable reading corner or an interesting science center. Also, capture examples of end products of projects the students have undertaken. Last, ask a colleague to take a few snapshots of you working with youngsters.

If you are attempting to change to another type of teaching assignment or a different role altogether, brainstorm the kinds of photos that would provide helpful information to your interviewer. For example, if you are hoping to move into the role of media specialist, you might want to include photos of a book celebration in which your youngsters dressed up as characters from children's literature and presented their books. If you wish to become an assistant administrator, a photograph of you working with parent volunteers might help your interviewer envision contributions you could make to the school.

Achievement Data

People reviewing your portfolio will be eager to see concrete evidence of your past successes. An impressive way to provide this proof is through achievement data. Include a few examples of your most impressive results concerning district, state, or national assessments. You may provide copies of data sheets you have been given concerning your students' performance, in which case you will need to black out student names, of course. Another option is to generate your own charts or graphs summarizing how your students have performed over time. Use different color type or highlighting to focus readers' attention on key parts of the lists, charts, or graphs you include.

Family and Community Involvement Activities

It is a good idea to provide a section of your portfolio showing how you have involved parents and community members in your past programs. For instance, you might include a couple of programs or fliers concerning events that involved families, such as student plays, science fairs, or family reading nights. Also consider generating a bulleted list of ways you might involve parents and others in the program you would offer in the new position you hope to acquire.

Fan Mail

Other artifacts that can convey to your interviewer information about your personality and your professional dedication are personal notes. Perhaps you have one or more treasured notes that you have received from students or parents. For instance, a child may have written you an end-of-the-year letter telling how he felt about working with you. A parent might have written to express excitement that his daughter developed an avid interest in history because of you. Notes such as these, included in your portfolio, help to round out the interviewer's impression of you.

Awards and Honors

Include information about awards, honors, or nominations that relate to previous or current teaching assignments. In a phrase, explain the nature of the award if it would not be familiar to people who will see your portfolio. Also include information about any awards that relate to the position to which you aspire. For instance, if you wish to transfer to a science teaching position in a departmentalized school, the administrator would like to know if you have had an article published in a science education publication.

WHAT TO LEAVE OUT

Chances are that no one will study your portfolio in depth. Considering how much time you will spend in putting it together, this sounds like discouraging news. It is not. Even if potential employers do not read every word of your portfolio, the mere fact that you have created one and obviously put much thought into the process will be impressive.

Just because an employer does not spend an hour studying your portfolio does not mean the document will not get proper attention. You will be using your portfolio as an important prop during your interview. (Techniques for doing so will be explained in Chapter 10.)

In preparing your portfolio, first focus on deciding what to put in and leave out by asking yourself, "What documents and items will convey information quickly and impressively?" For example, do not include artifacts that consist of pages of straight text. No one is going to have the time to read this material.

In addition, be very sure that everything you put into your portfolio accurately represents you as an educator. For example, do not include a reading comprehension handout that focuses exclusively on recall of details if you believe fostering higher levels of thinking in response to reading is crucial.

Last, do not clutter your portfolio with material that is redundant, with the exception of your résumé as already discussed. For instance, you can forgo including copies of your application or transfer form or letters of reference. However, carrying an extra copy of your résumé and letters of reference with you during an interview is a good idea. You then have the option of leaving the materials with the interviewer if an additional copy is needed for any reason.

A PACKAGE TO IMPRESS

The way you package your portfolio should say, "I am a classy, confident educator." Housing your portfolio in a good-looking, dignified binder will help you make this statement. A binder will be easier to manipulate at your interview than a folder. Choose a neutral, professional color, such as black, brown, gray, navy blue, or burgundy. Another option is to purchase a binder with a clear cover panel into which you can insert your own customized cover (see Figure 5.3 for an example).

Figure 5.3   Portfolio Cover

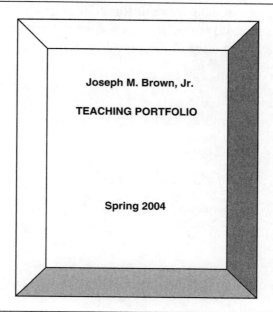

Joseph M. Brown, Jr.

TEACHING PORTFOLIO

Spring 2004

A table of contents should be included at the front. Index tabs are also a good idea so that you can quickly and easily find specific information during the interview. Use a good-quality white or ivory paper for the pages. Insert your photographs into plastic photo pages. As with all materials you prepare for this process, check and recheck for spelling or punctuation errors.

FINAL THOUGHTS

A portfolio is an excellent tool to have on hand as you go through the process of changing teaching assignments or applying for another role in education. Not everyone takes the time to prepare one, so having this additional resource on hand makes you stand out from the crowd. It also provides a concrete way of helping the interviewer envision who you are and what you will be able to accomplish if given the position you seek. Of course, achieving the goal of getting a good job without a portfolio *is* possible, but why not take time to give yourself this extra edge in a competitive job market?

Chapter Six

Getting the Interview

You will spend a lot of time preparing an impressive application or transfer request, résumé, and portfolio. If you simply send in this information without personal contact, however, your materials may not get the full attention they deserve.

MAKING PERSONAL CONTACT

You can follow a logical, effective plan for letting the appropriate people know that you have more than a passing interest in making a professional change. Make personal or phone contact . . . but do so in a way that is professional and effective.

When to Make Contact

Start making contact early. If you want to be successful in getting a change of position for the next school year, start working as soon as you have filled out a transfer form, which is in the late winter or very early spring in most systems.

Some school systems start to fill positions in the spring, while others are not ready until early summer. Making the contact early, however, gives you an edge even if people with whom you speak tell you that they are not yet interviewing.

If you are aspiring to a position that will be filled during the school year, begin your plan of action as soon as you hear about the vacancy. Even if the position has not yet been formally advertised, you can begin to let the right people know that you would like to be considered.

People to Contact

If you desire to change teaching assignments, the principal and assistant principal of a particular school where you would like to teach are crucial people to contact. Also, you should make yourself known to subject area or curriculum specialists if you are seeking a departmental position. Elementary programs often have elementary supervisors or specialists whom you can call on as well.

If you personally know someone who has "pull," you should contact him or her to say that you are looking for a position and would appreciate any leads. If this person offers to make a call and mention your name to someone who is hiring, that would be extremely helpful. Consider, however, whether this person is someone who agrees with you philosophically. If not, the strategy could backfire. For example, you may know a very fine teacher who is very traditional while you are very innovative. Having that person put in a good word for you could give the false impression that you, too, are traditional in your approach to education.

How to Make Contact

If you desire to change positions within your current school, you may be tempted to casually mention your interest to the principal when the opportunity arises. This strategy may be effective in some instances. To give more weight to the discussion and ensure that you have the administrator's undivided attention, however, consider scheduling an appointment to discuss your interest in a change of positions.

Personal contact is also an important strategy if you are interested in a position in a different school or district. Recognize that it is risky to stop by unannounced at a principal's or subject supervisor's office. This move can be viewed as presumptuous and can leave the bad impression that you do not respect how busy the person is. If you stop by uninvited, you put the principal or supervisor in the uncomfortable position of taking time away from scheduled work or being an "ogre" and sending you away. In either case, you risk a negative first impression.

It is much safer to make initial contact by phone call. Choose the time of day carefully. Some possibilities are before students arrive in the morning or after they leave in the afternoon. Even then, principals often have meetings, but you stand a better chance than trying to make contact during the hectic school day. Attempting to reach administrators and supervisors on days when they are on duty, but students are not in attendance, is helpful. For instance, teacher training days or snow days in late winter are possibilities. Not only are administrators likely to be able to answer the phone, but they may also be less stressed and able to concentrate more fully on your call.

Nature of the Contact

An important consideration when you call a principal or subject area supervisor is to respect the person's time by keeping your call short. Let the person know you are an experienced teacher and state what kind of change you are interested in making. Say a few words about why you are interested in the particular school or district. If you have a contact known to the person whom you are calling and who has agreed to endorse your efforts, diplomatically drop the person's name during the conversation. The following sample gives an idea of how your phone conversation might go.

Sample Phone Contact Conversation

You: Mr. Smith, I am sure you are very busy so I will be brief. I am Lee Brown and I have three years of experience teaching third grade. Mrs. Jones suggested I give you a call to let you know I have just gotten my master's degree in reading and am interested in a reading specialist position.

Principal Smith: Okay.

You: She said that your specialist is retiring at the end of the school year. I would like to be considered for that position. I have heard a lot of good things about your Raring to Read program from teachers in your school, and I think I could contribute to it.

Principal Smith: Well, I appreciate your interest, but you will have to apply and go through the district process.

You: Yes, I will do that as soon as the announcement comes out. In the meantime, I would like to send you a résumé to keep in your files so you can see the kinds of experiences I have had.

Principal Smith: Yes, that would be fine.

You: Thank you for your time. I hope I will hear from you a little later in the spring.

If you try to reach a principal or supervisor and the secretary says the person is not available, it is usually not the most effective route to leave a message. Many will not have the time or motivation to call back given all the urgent business on their agendas. As an alternative, try to establish a positive rapport with the secretary and ask when a good time to reach the principal or supervisor might be. Then, try at that time and remind the secretary of the suggestion to call. Whether you leave a message or try the alternative strategy, keep trying. Be persistent in calling back, but be *extremely and genuinely* polite, understanding, and considerate when you do.

Written Follow-Up

After you have had phone contact with a principal or supervisor, follow up in writing. Send your résumé and a note mentioning your call. Do this promptly so the person may still remember you and be impressed with your follow-through. An example of such a letter follows.

Sample Follow-Up Letter After Phone Contact

Lee Brown
23 Church Street
Ellicott City, Maryland 00000

Mr. Jonathan B. Smith
Principal, Lincoln Elementary
4678 Route 98
Lincoln Heights, Maryland 00000

Dear Mr. Smith:

Thank you for taking the time to speak to me on the telephone yesterday. As I mentioned, I am very interested in the reading specialist position in your school.

My résumé and a sample reading comprehension lesson that I used with my third graders is enclosed with this note. I am also including information about my classroom reading incentive program, which is somewhat similar to your Raring to Read program. These materials will

---

(Continued)

(Continued)

> provide additional information about my experience and qualifications.
>
> I hope to hear from you once your hiring process gets underway. I can be reached at 555–1212. Good luck with your Raring to Read program.
>
> Sincerely,
> Lee Brown

As shown in the foregoing example, sending a work sample to give the principal or supervisor a concrete picture of what you can do is a worthwhile idea. See if you can send the person something that relates to your phone conversation or anything that connects with the school's programs. If you have a particularly impressive letter of reference, that could also be included. Once again, use professional stationery and envelopes as discussed in relation to application cover letters and résumés.

WHEN PERSONAL CONTACT IS IMPOSSIBLE

If for some reason, you reach a total dead end after repeated attempts to make phone contact, do not despair. In addition to the materials you have sent to personnel, mail personalized packets to relevant principals and subject area supervisors.

Prepare a copy of your résumé for the mail packet. Consider sending a lesson plan, unit plan, or some other evidence of your educational approach and your attention to detail. As with the follow-up packet described earlier, an outstanding letter of reference may be included. You will also need a cover letter. The same basic guidelines can be followed as explained in Chapter 3 concerning the cover letter for your application. Find a way to personalize this communication to the principal or supervisor to whom you are sending your résumé, however. The following sample may provide some ideas to help you get started.

Sample Letter Without Phone Contact

Pat Ritter
1480 Democracy Boulevard
Hagerstown, Maryland 00000

Dr. Melinda Bower
Supervisor of Elementary Education
Hagerstown School District
98032 Key Highway
Hagerstown, Maryland 00000

Dear Dr. Bower:

I am interested in a primary grade teaching position in an elementary school in your district. I have had five years of teaching experience in first grade at Sunny Spring Elementary in Frederick, Maryland. My past experiences have made me aware of the importance of an integrated approach to reading instruction. I have been successful in using a program that integrates phonics, literature, and writing. I understand that Hagerstown School District uses a similar approach.

The enclosed résumé and sample lesson plan that I have used with my slower developing readers will give you additional information about my teaching approach. I am also enclosing a letter of reference from my current principal. After you have had a chance to look at these materials, I would like an opportunity to discuss with you my qualifications and find out what positions are available.

I hope to hear from you soon. I can be reached at 555–1212.

Sincerely,
Pat Ritter

You may decide to drop off the materials at the principal's or supervisor's office instead of mailing them. In view of what has already been said about unannounced visits, do not go with the expectation of talking with the person to whom you are addressing the packet. Do, however, dress the part of the professional even for this brief visit to the building. Be extremely and genuinely courteous to the secretary when you request that the materials be given to the administrator. If you put your best foot forward, the secretary will be more likely to remember you and be helpful when you make follow-up contact at a later date.

STAYING IN TOUCH

"Whew!" you might say when the materials have reached their destination. Now, you may think you can relax and wait for that all-important call. Wrong! You will need to periodically check in with the supervisors and principals to whom you have sent materials. You will need to remind them, in a way that is not pushy or annoying, that you are still available and interested. Occasional calls and brief notes can serve this purpose. The following is an example of the kind of note you might send.

Example of a Reminder Note

Lee Brown
23 Church Street
Ellicott City, Maryland 00000

Mr. Jonathan B. Smith
Principal, Lincoln Elementary
4678 Route 98
Lincoln Heights, Maryland 00000

Dear Mr. Smith:

In April, I spoke with you briefly about my interest in the reading specialist position at your school. You may

---

recall that I also sent you a packet about my education and experience.

Now that the announcement of the position has been posted, I want to let you know that I am still very eager to work in your school. Since my last contact with you, I have been volunteering on Saturdays at the reading clinic associated with Maryland College. I am enjoying the experience and finding it very helpful in giving me a chance to help students solve many kinds of reading problems. I am eager to apply what I am learning to a full-time reading position.

I look forward to the possibility of an interview with you. I can be reached at 555–1212.

Sincerely,
Lee Brown

Repeat your telephone number each time you leave a phone message or write a note. Administrators are busy, and they need to be able to contact you without taking extra time to search for your number.

SCHEDULING THE INTERVIEW

After all your hard preparation work, the exciting day will come when you are called and invited to be interviewed for the position to which you aspire. When you get the call, be as accommodating as possible about scheduling the interview. Sometimes, meeting job candidates is scheduled for only a narrow window of time, such as one day or one morning. Principals and other interviewers are busy people. They usually need to confine their interview appointments within a limited time frame so that they can get a particular position filled and move on to the next task. Reshuffle anything and everything you already had planned for the specified day so that you can accommodate the interviewer's schedule. The person who is requesting to meet with you wants to see immediately that you are committed to do whatever it takes. Do not hesitate to say an enthusiastic, "Yes," when an interview date is presented to you.

If you have a choice of interview times, the last time slot is considered the best with the first being almost as desirable. Do not worry, however, if you land somewhere in the middle of the schedule. You will be so well prepared that you will impress the administrator no matter when you interview. However, given a choice, pick last or first.

If you are not familiar with the person with whom you will be interviewing, confirm and write down his or her name and title before hanging up the phone. If the office where you will meet is new to you, get the exact location and directions before you end the conversation. Also, verify the meeting time before signing off. These may seem like obvious points, and in your calmer moments, you would undoubtedly handle these details. However, when the call comes in, you will be excited. Jot down all the specifics so you do not have to call back and ask for information to be repeated.

FINAL THOUGHTS

Personal contact is possibly the most important strategy in getting an interview. It requires courage, diplomacy, and persistence. Administrators understand that getting a job is important to you. If you are very careful to be respectful of their time and come across as wanting them to know that you are still interested, as opposed to coming across as demanding, they will be impressed with your perseverance.

CHAPTER SEVEN

Doing Your Homework

O nce you have successfully scheduled one or more interviews, another stage of the process of getting the job you want is ahead of you. You need to get busy doing your homework. The more thought and preparation you put into getting ready for the interview, the more impressed your interviewers will be and the more relaxed you will feel. You will be able to use the short amount of time allotted to each applicant to your best advantage so the interviewers will get a good picture of your willingness and ability to handle the position to which you aspire.

MATERIALS TO STUDY

If you are seeking a teaching job at a different grade level or focusing on a different subject area than you have taught before, an important document to obtain is the curriculum guide for the position for which you are interviewing. You should be able to borrow one from another teacher, your principal, or the content area supervisor. Study this material so you will be familiar with the content and approach it describes. Anticipate questions that may be asked. Consider how you would implement the curriculum, and jot down concrete examples of what you would do so that you will have these in mind when you are interviewed.

If you are attempting to get a teaching or administrative position in another school or district, request materials from both the school and relevant central office curriculum departments. Ask for handbooks, newsletters, or other materials that highlight important goals and programs. Studying these materials will help you know what is important to the particular school and community and why. This knowledge will assist you in thinking of specific ways you can support the goals and contribute to the programs. Of course, if you are applying for a position in your current school, you will already be familiar with this information. However, team newsletters or subject area publications might fill in your background if you are attempting to transfer to another grade level or subject area.

TALKING WITH PEOPLE

Teachers who work in the school where you wish to transfer or in the subject area or level you wish to teach can be valuable resources during the homework phase. The issues and challenges related to the job you wish to have may be different from those associated with your current teaching assignment. Identify people you know personally or ask friends to connect you with appropriate colleagues who can help you become aware of topics of discussion that may come up in the interview. If the position you are seeking is a specialist or administrative job, talking to a cross section of people representing various grades and levels within the school will provide valuable information. Parents and community members can also shed light on important concerns and goals of a particular school or program.

During the interview, you may have an opportunity to mention that you have talked with people about important issues related to the job. This information will provide evidence of your enthusiasm and initiative.

PREPARING FOR INTERVIEW QUESTIONS

If you have taught elementary reading, you have helped children develop and use prediction skills. You have asked students to use their background knowledge to surmise from book titles, illustrations, and other elements what a book will address. Now you need to use prediction skills yourself. Your interview will be much less stressful and much more success-ful if you spend some time looking into your crystal ball and imagining the questions that may come up in the interview. You should be able to predict interview topics fairly accu-rately and use this information to think through the kinds of responses and examples you may give. Rather than having to answer the questions "off the cuff" when you are in a stressful situation, you can take time to carefully ponder your beliefs and practices in the peace and calm of your home before the spotlight is on you.

The following general topics are commonly addressed during interviews for teaching, specialist, and assistant princi-pal positions:

- Your background
- Current approaches
- Student developmental levels
- Effective lesson elements
- Behavior management
- Grading and assessment
- Parent and community involvement
- Professional strengths and weaknesses
- Questions concerning the job

This section will help you think through possible answers and responses. It will not, of course, dictate answers since those must come from your own beliefs and experiences.

Your Background

The background question is usually the opening one in an interview. It is meant as an icebreaker to try to relax the applicant. Although the response you give will probably repeat information in your résumé and application or transfer form, your answer will give your interviewers a chance to refresh their memory of what they have read about you.

In some senses, this question is an easy one. The information you share should be very familiar to you since it is your history. In another sense, however, the question can be tricky. It is not a "throw away" even though it is basically designed to get the ball rolling. You can use it to your advantage to immediately give the impression of someone who is ready and eager to undertake a new challenge in your career. You have to consider the following:

- What few things about my background are most pertinent to the position?

     You will not have time to share you entire life history, nor is your entire personal and professional history relevant. Pick out three to five important bits of information that would lead an interviewer to believe you are prepared to be successful in the job.

- How can I impress the interviewer with the breadth and depth of my experience without droning on and on?

     Plan to quickly touch on any of your qualifications that you hold in common with most or all of the other applicants. Allocate a little more time to anything that makes you stand out from the crowd.

- In what ways can I begin to reveal the positive aspects of my personality as I answer this question?

     A little of your sense of humor may come through as you start into the interview. Perhaps the enthusiasm with which you explain how you have prepared yourself for the position will also be evident as you address the first question.

- How can I organize my response in a way that makes sense and does not jump around?

  You could share information in chronological order. As an alternative, you could organize the tidbits you share by order of importance, being sure that the most impressive parts are at the beginning and end of the response. A third option is sharing by category: for example, telling about a few relevant work experiences and then a couple of examples of specialized training that have prepared you for the job.

You might want to begin by jotting notes about your background on a mind map such as the one shown in Figure 7.1 to help you think through this question.

Since this question is just the hors d'oeuvre to the main body of the interview, you want to provide a meaningful answer without eating up too many minutes of your interview. It is more important to save plenty of time to answer other questions in depth.

Current Approaches

Interview questions related to approaches can vary widely based on who is doing the interviewing, how progressive or back to basics the school district is, and the type of position you

Figure 7.1   Sample Mind Map

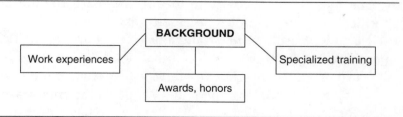

are seeking to obtain. Subject area supervisors will generally provide the most in-depth questions on this topic. In most cases, principals will ask more general content questions since they cannot be expected to be experts in all subjects and grades.

The situation can be a bit trickier if the principal taught the subject or grade you aspire to teach. Your interviewer may not be up-to-date on the latest innovations in your particular area of expertise. On the other hand, the person may be very up-to-date and have very strong opinions about the proper approach to the content area. It is a plus if you can find out through the grapevine what the administrator taught back in his or her classroom days so you can be especially respectful of that background while showing what you know about current innovations.

If you have previously taught the subject for which you are applying, be ready to explain how you have approached the content, and be prepared to reference the most important research and theory that support your content approach. If you are preparing to step out and teach a subject area that is new to you, go back to the curriculum guide you borrowed to ensure that you are ready for questions in this area. Be especially wary if you taught the content area at one point but have not done so recently. It is astounding how much change can occur in just a few years. If you come into an interview talking about how you taught a subject area five years ago, you may be talking yourself out of a job.

As you think about how you will answer content approach questions, consider cross-curricular district-level trends as well. For instance, the district may be focusing on high-level thinking skills or multiple intelligences. Prepare to discuss how you would support these initiatives within your content approach.

The most important advice in this area is to plan to be specific. Think of examples of lessons or materials you have used or might use that illustrate your content approach. The interviewers want to be convinced that not only can you discuss current approaches, but you can use them effectively, also. Do not take the risk of assuming that your past experience will speak for itself. Be explicit.

Student Developmental Levels

Preparing for questions about developmental characteristics of the students you wish to teach is crucial if you wish to change grade levels. You may have years of impressive experience as a fifth grade teacher. If you wish to move to a first grade position, however, you need to show the interviewer that you understand that primary youngsters need help wiping their noses and tying their shoes before they can concentrate on your captivating mathematics lesson.

If you are venturing into a new grade level, talk with friends and relatives who have children that age. Glance through child development books. Be ready to show the interviewer that you know the joys and challenges of the age and that you have concrete plans for capitalizing on the former and overcoming the latter.

Effective Lesson Elements

No matter how seasoned a teacher you are, you will likely be asked a question designed to show that you take planning seriously and have the skills needed to create effective long-range and short-range lesson and unit plans. A building administrator may use a question such as the following to assess your subject area knowledge along with your planning technique.

Typical Lesson Plan Format Questions

- If I came into your classroom, what might a lesson look like?
- Give an example of a lesson you have taught.
- What is the best (or a favorite) lesson you taught and tell why you think so?
- How would you adapt a lesson to meet individual needs?
- What elements would you be looking for in observing a lesson? (for assistant principal applicants)

Admittedly, these questions are quite nebulous. When you are under pressure, it is hard to cook up an idea on the spot or to remember *any* lesson you ever taught, let alone an impressive one. Take time during this planning stage to select a lesson in your subject or grade level and think how you would describe it. If possible, pick one that has some relationship to the position for which you are applying. Consider comments you could make about how this lesson could be adapted. Even if the lesson plan you have prepared does not exactly match the planning question you are asked in the interview, it will be easier to modify than to start from scratch. Also keep in mind that it can be very effective to simply turn to the pages in your portfolio with the sample lesson and talk through it, pointing out the areas you have highlighted.

In collecting your thoughts about this kind of question, be sure to include all the elements of a standard lesson plan. As a seasoned teacher, you may do some of the steps so automatically that you are tempted to gloss over them in the interview. Do not give in to this temptation. Your interviewer will want evidence that you are detailed and thorough in your planning.

Behavior Management

The issue of classroom management is near and dear to the hearts of principals. After all, they are the ones who have to deal with unruly students and irate parents when teachers lack positive, effective management skills. It is possible that if principals could ask only one question in an interview, they would choose one about classroom management.

This question may be asked in an open-ended manner, such as, "What techniques do you find helpful in keeping students on task?" With this type of inquiry, the interviewer is attempting to see if you have a well thought out plan for establishing expectations right from the first day of school. The interviewer also wants to hear you discuss explicit techniques, such as moving closer to students who are off task. You would do well to include ideas about involving parents in the positive and negative aspects of classroom behavior. In addition, think about how you can construct your response to show that you know the difference between situations that you should handle and those in which administrators should be involved.

Again, the temptation will be to leave out techniques that are second nature to you because you have been successfully employing them for years. However, thinking about and preparing to discuss these techniques is extremely important, particularly if the person interviewing you has not observed your teaching. Depending on how the question is worded, you may be able to turn to the relevant page in your portfolio and use it to structure and illustrate your response.

Another approach to classroom management questions is for the interviewer to present a scenario. An example is provided below, but predicting the content of this type of question is impossible because each interviewer who uses this strategy puts a unique twist on it.

Example of Classroom Management Scenario Question

You have just instructed the class to read a section of a text and complete a related task. Johnny loudly slams his book shut and says, "I'm not readin' that stupid story!" What do you do?

Even though this question appears to be more specific and concrete than the open-ended question, it is still relatively nebulous. There are lots of details left out. Many interviewees might become flustered by not knowing more about the context. Was this routine behavior for Johnny? How did the other students react? What was going on in Johnny's home life?

In answering the question, simply fill in those details to suit yourself as you go along. You might say, "Let us assume that Johnny has never done anything like this before. He is usually very cooperative, therefore, I would . . . " If the interviewer stops you and says, "No, let us assume that Johnny is a chronic behavior problem," then play along in that direction.

The interviewer wants to see that you can go through a multi-step process, so it is not to your advantage to say, "I just went over to Johnny and talked to him quietly, and he apologized." Make it more complex so that you can show that you have a range of sophisticated techniques in your classroom management repertoire, including enlisting parental support. The classroom management section of your portfolio may be a valuable prop as you answer this question.

If you are applying to move into a grade level other than that which you are currently teaching, be sure to discuss techniques appropriate to that level. What works with first graders is very different from approaches that keep upper elementary students on task. Just because you have demonstrated ability in one grade level does not mean that the principal will automatically assume you can handle the behavior challenges that are involved in other grade levels.

Grading and Assessment

The issues of grading and assessment may be handled together or separately. Concerning assessment, you may simply be asked how you would evaluate progress. In that case, you can share information about formal and informal assessment approaches you have used or would use. Interviewees frequently make the mistake of being vague on this point. Be ready to share at least a few concrete examples while also showing that you are eager to learn and implement any assessment practices that are unique to the grade or school into which you wish to transfer.

Some districts use certain standardized assessments with particular grades. If you are attempting to move into one of those grades, learn about these tests before coming to the interview. For example, find out whether the assessments are multiple choice or performance tasks. Talk to colleagues who have prepared students for these assessments. Even if you do not have direct experience with certain assessments that will be required, your interviewers will be impressed that you are taking this responsibility seriously by finding out about them in advance. It will strengthen your interview considerably if you can mention a specific way or two that you plan to support success on these measures. Remember that not only are assessments useful teaching tools, but their results are seen as very public statements about the success of a particular school.

You must be ready to address the topic of grading in a concrete and logical way as well. If you are attempting to transfer to a different school, it would be helpful to talk to teachers you know in that school about any mandated grading policies. If you are able to gather this information, you can then think about whether your past grading practices can be used in the new situation. If not, determine how you might modify them. If you do not have access to this information, you will simply have to prepare to discuss what you have done in the past and explain the thinking behind your practices. Plan to preface your remarks by saying that you will describe the grading approach you have used in the past but are ready to find out how the school handles grading and how you can tailor your ideas to be consistent with those requirements.

Mainly, your interviewers will want to be convinced that you operate logically in this area. They want to be assured that you would not be nebulous or arbitrary with grading, thereby arousing student confusion and parent concern.

Parent and Community Involvement

Interviews for positions in education frequently include a question about parental involvement. Often, this comes near the end of the discussion. Many interviewees do not anticipate this query and offer a vague response. If you prepare some thoughts in advance, you can score extra points by being more concrete and creative than most. Think of a few specific examples that directly relate to the subject and grade you wish to teach. These may fall into categories such as the following:

- Creative ways to include parents in instructional activities
- Opportunities for family members to share their areas of expertise relative to jobs, travel, or hobbies

- Interesting examples of homework assignments that involve family members
- Techniques for communicating positive accomplishments to parents

Spend a few moments thinking of two or three innovative ideas to share if this question is asked. A well thought out response will help the interviewer see that you know the value of a teacher-parent team effort and that you have ideas above and beyond asking parents to chaperone field trips.

Professional Strengths and Weaknesses

Many interviewers wind up their questioning by asking, "What is your main strength and weakness?" The tendency is for this to be more or less a throwaway question. That is, applicants are seldom hired or rejected based on their response. Furthermore, the second part of the question necessitates, if not a lie, at least a fabrication.

If you encounter this question, avoid responding with a typical answer such as, "My greatest strength is that I get along well with people." Think what kind of statement you can make that sets you apart from other applicants. For instance, if you grew up in the district in which you are applying, your knowledge of the community might be a strong asset.

Concerning a weakness, the common practice is to avoid the truth. Imagine your interviewer's reaction if you blatantly announced, "I cannot seem to kick my smoking habit," or "My spelling is atrocious. It took three friends just to help me get my résumé looking presentable."

Instead of revealing a true weakness, people generally try to contrive a response that sounds like a weakness on the surface but that actually could be perceived as a benefit to the employer. The most common answer is some variation on the theme, "My greatest weakness is that I am a workaholic (or perfectionist). I just work all of the time."

You might take another approach with this question. Think of a *former* weakness and say a few words about how you overcame it. For example, "I used to have a weakness in relation to organization. Then, I read everything I could get my hands on about time management and learned how to set priorities and budget my time. Now, I am able to get a lot done in a short amount of time." Think this through as you plan for your interview. What for many is a throwaway question can be one more opportunity for you to impress your interviewer.

Questions Concerning the Job

At the very end of the conversation, interviewers almost always ask, "Do you have any questions?" Most applicants say something diplomatic, such as, "I think you have answered all my questions. I cannot think of anything else." At this point, the response is probably true for most people. They are so tired and grateful to be getting out of the hot seat that they truly cannot think of any questions. If you have prepared ahead, however, this ending query will give you a chance to leave a favorable final impression. This segment of the interview can be like an after-dinner mint that caps off the whole experience.

People like to talk about themselves, so a question about the interviewer's philosophy on an aspect of education is a good idea. However, avoid sounding as if you are interviewing the interviewer. Another approach is to ask a question that gives you a chance to reveal something extra you would like to do if given the position for which you are applying.

Examples of Questions You Might Ask

- What is your main goal for the school (program) next year?
- I have a drama background. Would there be any possibility of my working with all the fifth grade classes to put on an end-of-the-year play if I transferred to that grade?
- I have an idea for a mathematics fair. Would that be something I might eventually be able to work toward if I were on the faculty of this school?

REHEARSING FOR YOUR INTERVIEW

Thinking through ideas in your head does not necessarily guarantee that you will be able to communicate those ideas verbally in a clear, complete, and succinct way. Even though you may feel awkward at first, the best thing you can do is ask a friend, preferably a teaching colleague or a family member, to help you rehearse. Give the person the list of questions you predict you may be asked and have your friend or family member ask them.

Make this situation as real as possible. Do some of your practice sitting in a chair at a table rather than just lounging on the sofa. Actually, practice how you would come in and greet the interviewer. Become accustomed to getting materials, such as your portfolio, notepad, and pen, out of your carrying case and arranging them conveniently on the table so that you can do this smoothly to avoid fumbling around and making yourself nervous.

Even though you have been standing before a class with poise and confidence for years and, perhaps, have given presentations to colleagues, do not be tempted to skip this step. You probably have not been in an interview situation for a long time. You will have to contend with the normal feelings of discomfort at being in this circumstance. The more you can get the logistics on automatic pilot, the more you will be able to focus on the quality of your responses.

Realize that the first time or two you run through your rehearsal, your answers are likely to be choppy and halting. That is why you are practicing. As your partner goes over the questions with you a few times, you will work out smooth, natural ways of responding.

As an alternative or addition to live rehearsals, you can also tape-record your responses and then listen to see how you sound. Looking into a mirror and rehearsing is also helpful for some people. Although rehearsal is strongly recommended, avoid overdoing it. You do not want your responses to sound canned.

LOCATION, LOCATION

If you are attempting to transfer to a new location or are meeting at a district office, be very, very sure that you know where you are going. Call for directions or consult a map or www.mapquest.com. This advice sounds obvious, yet a surprising number of applicants do not take this step. They end up lost or misjudging the travel time and arrive at their interview distracted and distressed or, worse yet, late, which is certainly not the impression you want to make after all your careful preparation.

FINAL THOUGHTS

Seeing a teacher who has the qualifications and determination to succeed in a new position fail in an interview because of responding to key questions with statements such as "I never thought about that" is heartbreaking. This really happens. Do not let it happen to you.

Your interview is a major factor in getting the job you want. Putting serious effort into predicting and preparing for questions related to that job is a tremendous help. Rehearsing your ideas aloud will also give you an extra advantage once the big day comes.

Chapter Eight

What to Wear, What to Wear?

A t first glance, some readers may be insulted by the idea of tips for an interview outfit. You may be saying, "I am an adult and a professional. I dress myself perfectly fine everyday." That is true. It is also true, however, that what makes sense as a teaching outfit is not necessarily the same as what makes sense for an interview. Furthermore, it has probably been a long time since you had to appear for an interview, so it might be worthwhile to make sure that you are up-to-date on today's standards and expectations. Planning an interview outfit can be fun and may give you an excuse to treat yourself to a new article of clothing or an accessory to make the day of your interview even more special.

OUTFIT IMPACT

People should be judged on what they can do, not on their appearance. Don't you wish that were true? The fact is that appearance *does* make a difference. Putting some thought into how you will dress for your interview is one more way to convey to your interviewer that you take pride in yourself and your profession. Even if you will be interviewing with your current administrator or another person whom you know personally, you have a chance to show a facet of your image that people do not see everyday. While planning an outfit with impact is a plus, being decked out in a several-hundred-dollar power suit is not necessary. The following sections will help you think about options.

Women's Interview Outfits

For women, an outfit made up of a classic skirt suit or pantsuit or a dress with a jacket works well. If you are good at mix and match, you could also put together a professional-looking outfit that consists of a jacket, skirt or tailored pants, and a blouse.

Although neutrals such as black, navy, tan, or gray help convey a professional image, you do not have to restrict yourself to these. Choose a color that is flattering to you. While you do not want to appear bland and mousy, you also want to avoid anything too loud and distracting. Save the lime green outfit for another occasion. In addition to color, be sure nothing else about the outfit will be distracting to the interviewer or to you during your meeting. For example, be sure your skirt is long and loose enough so that you will not have to be tugging at it when you want to put all your focus on the interview questions.

In addition to conveying the image of professionalism and confidence, you also want your interviewers to understand that you are a person who attends to details. Your outfit can help you say that. Skillful use of accessories is the trick. Well-polished classic shoes, some tasteful jewelry or an interesting scarf, and a nice leather belt will underline the impression of you as a person who dots her "i's" and crosses her "t's."

Once you have decided on your outfit, try on all the pieces. Be sure you feel comfortable and confident. The interview is your day to shine. Take full advantage of it.

Men's Interview Outfits

For men, a suit or a nice jacket or blazer and slacks will convey professionalism. A classic style in a neutral color or subtle pattern is a good choice. Wear a white or pastel, long-sleeved shirt, and top off your outfit with a classy tie. Select a quiet pattern, such as subtle stripes. For a man, a tie is the signature piece. For an interview, it should say, "Responsible, mature, trustworthy, and serious." Leave the Snoopy tie in the closet until you get the transfer or promotion. The students will love it, but the interviewers may not. Attend to details such as polishing your shoes and being sure your clothing is well pressed. No doubt, you have told your students, "Neatness counts" as they have prepared to hand in major assignments. The same is true for interviews.

CARRYING CASE

A professional-looking carrying case is an important final touch for both men and women interviewees. This accessory makes a great first impression as you walk into the interview room. As a teacher, you probably have one or more trusty tote bags that you lug around. Leave them at home and see if you can borrow a nice leather case from someone if you do not own one.

Be sure the size is one that you can handle easily. Avoid anything that might be awkward or hard to maneuver. Do not overpack your case. Rather, place in it the essential tools and props you will need in your interview. Be sure they are well organized so that you do not have to fumble around to find what you need. The most important items to include are an 8½ by 11-inch notepad and a classy pen. Also have a manila folder with an extra copy of your résumé and letters of reference in case the interviewer needs these. Of course, your portfolio also needs to go into your case. Some people have had good results from packing one or two books that they know are current and important in their subject area. While a bit contrived, this strategy does show that you are aware of the latest information.

A special recommendation for women is to consider leaving your purse in the car and simply carrying the case. The benefit is that you will have less luggage to juggle when you are trying to look cool, calm, and collected. If you do this, put an extra set of car keys in the case the night before the interview. You will be glad you took this step in the event that you get nervous on the day of the appointment and inadvertently lock your main key set in the car.

FINAL THOUGHTS

Regardless of how much we wish people were judged by what is in their heads and hearts instead of what is on their backs, it pays to be realistic. Your interview attire will provide an immediate first impression. You want it to create an impression of confidence and professionalism that you will then proceed to confirm with the way you participate in the interview conversation.

Never make the mistake of thinking you can dress casually for an interview, even if you know the interviewer well, or for some reason, think that you have the job already. Put your best foot forward, in a professional-looking shoe, of course, and let everything about you say, "Competence."

CHAPTER NINE

Get Set for Outstanding Interview Performance

Y ou may be as serene as a yoga instructor when you face your students on a day-to-day basis. Your calm, collected demeanor can easily turn to nervous anxiety as the day of your interview approaches, however. The last-minute jitters are normal, even if you have followed every suggestion in Chapters 1 through 8 of this book. There are some steps you can take in the days immediately preceding the interview to help lower your stress level. Try any of the following that you think might be beneficial for you.

RELAX YOUR BODY

Your mind is going to be the star of the show when it comes to the interview; however, you know that there is a mind-body connection. If you are totally worn out and stressed out, your mind will not be at its sharpest. As you go through the mental exercise of preparing for your interview, do your best to squeeze in at least a short period of time to exercise in the days preceding your appointment. This may mean simply taking a fifteen-minute walk each day.

Also, think about supporting your mind-body connection by eating foods that are good for you and avoiding excess amounts of those that are not. Watch your consumption of sugar, caffeine, and alcohol as you prepare for your big day.

RELAX YOUR MIND

If you are like most people, you perform better when your mind is relatively relaxed. In the days preceding the interview, use whatever means generally work for you to set up a relaxed state of mind. Try to plan out the few days before the interview so you are not dashing around in a frenzy but rather have time for some soothing activities. This can be particularly challenging if your interview is scheduled while school is still in session, as opposed to during the summer. If that is the case, think about creating lesson plans for your class that will not keep you up until 11:00 p.m. assembling materials or grading papers. You can still provide the high-quality program you always offer, but keep your workload in mind, too. (Some of the tips in *Sweating the Small Stuff* and the lesson plans in *Timesaving Tips for Teachers* may help you be ultra-efficient during this time.)

Use some of the time you save with your streamlined lesson plans the few days before your interview to do a few relaxing activities. Take an hour to engage in pursuits you enjoy, such as reading, listening to music, or watching television. Make personal or phone contact with supportive friends and family members. Treat yourself to a few days of avoiding contact with people who you usually associate with tense feelings.

Of course, if you have a spouse and children, you will need to elicit their help. Consider having a brief family meeting in which you explain how important your goal of a transfer or promotion is. Be explicit about telling your family the kinds of support you will need from them for a while.

The days before an interview are a good time to keep in focus any spiritual practices that have meaning for you. If it fits into your belief system, pray and ask like-minded family and friends to add their thoughts to your cause. You might find it more peace producing to pray that the outcome will be the one that is best for your career rather than a "Please, please, *please,* God, I will do anything you want if I can only have this job" type of prayer. If you also find meaning in spiritual exercises such as journaling, imaging, or meditating, call on these practices, too. For example, close your eyes and mentally picture yourself being relaxed and doing well during your interview conversation.

The days preceding an interview are not necessarily the ideal time to start brand new habits. It does, however, make sense to schedule time to do things that have brought you peace and comfort in the past. Subjecting yourself to an interview is a courageous thing to do. Appreciate yourself for taking this step and treat yourself extra well.

Putting any single interview into perspective is important. You may well go through several before you get the results you want. Do the best you can, but do not consider any specific interview to be a life-or-death event.

THE EVENING BEFORE

Take special care with planning your activities the evening before your interview. Do your best to get any schoolwork done before you leave school, or at least finish any home tasks as early as possible. Try to plan a peaceful evening with family or friends who are optimistic and relaxing. Do not tax yourself with elaborate meal preparations unless that is relaxing for you.

Guard against overeating or drinking. This is not the night for you to spend with your stomach fighting the pizza you had for dinner. Plan to get a full eight hours of sleep and set your alarm a half-hour early so you will not feel rushed in the morning. Give your outfit and carrying case a final check, so you do not have to deal with any last-minute stressful surprises. End your evening with something soothing, such as a cup of tea or time to read from a favorite book.

THE DAY OF THE INTERVIEW

You will probably have no control over whether the interview takes place on a day when you are teaching or not. Either situation can be an advantage. If your interview is on a nonteaching day, you do not have to worry about getting chalk dust on your interview outfit or getting stressed by classroom situations you may have to handle. On the other hand, having your interview on a school day can be a benefit in that working will take your mind off the appointment.

Allow yourself a little extra time to get to the interview location. If you have to drive, consider listening to music that soothes you or an amusing CD as one last way to relax yourself. Breathe deeply and calmly to prepare yourself for a positive experience.

FINAL THOUGHTS

Doing a thoroughly professional job of preparing for an interview takes a lot of work. Honor all your efforts by being sure to take good care of yourself those final days and hours before the big event. Realize that the people who love you will support your efforts and be glad to help if you are straightforward about what you need from them.

A Successful Interview

F rom the minute you walk into the interview room, you will begin to implement your plan for success. Your outfit will be working for you and you will have all the materials you need. You may surprise yourself by actually having fun with the interview conversation once you get started.

OFF AND RUNNING

Project your confidence immediately by making eye contact and extending your hand for a firm handshake. Take the initiative of breaking the ice by saying something such as, "Good morning, Mr. Smith. The directions your secretary gave me were great. It was easy to find your building." As you settle into the seat offered to you, quickly prepare your interview space without appearing to take over. Open your case and take out your portfolio, notepad, and pen. Close your case, and put it on the floor out of your way.

RULES OF THE GAME

As the interviewer begins, listen attentively to any rules and parameters that are set up. You need to be aware that interviewers are very concerned about providing consistency in an attempt to ensure equity. Therefore, every interviewee may be asked exactly the same questions in exactly the same way. This situation can make the interview seem rigid and formal since the person or people asking questions may not be asking follow-up questions or adding any pleasantries or feedback. Just be aware that if your interview has a formal tone, it is not because the interviewer is not warming up to or appreciating you. Take it in stride and continue to be your engaging self.

Also, some interviewers assign point values to questions and grade each response. The person who gets the highest score theoretically gets the job. If you use the planning steps described in this book and follow the guidelines in the next section about answering questions, this situation can be a plus rather than a minus for you.

Last, keep in mind that interviews are usually scheduled for a specific amount of time. They are not open-ended conversations. Commonly, each interview is allocated thirty or forty-five minutes. Either the next applicant will be coming in after you, or the interviewer will have other responsibilities that need attention. Keep time parameters in mind as you judge how long to spend on each question.

ANSWERING QUESTIONS

Your main task in the interview, of course, will be to listen carefully to questions the interviewer asks and respond. That sounds simple given that you have already thought about what and how you want to communicate concerning your experience and approach. However, you will still need to be careful to avoid the five most common pitfalls.

Potential Pitfalls

- Straying from the question
- Rambling on and on
- Being excessively brief
- Speaking in generalities
- Making assumptions

Be Direct

Listen with great care to each question. Jotting down a few words on your notepad to remind yourself of the question is perfectly acceptable and even looked on favorably. This practice is particularly helpful if the question has several parts. For example, "How would you include parents in your program? How would you recruit them? What kinds of tasks would you have them do, and how would you keep them motivated?"

If you do not fully understand the question, ask for clarification. For instance, if the interviewer asks, "Describe what I would see if I observed your reading class," you might need to ask, "Does the school prescribe whether basal texts or trade books are used?"

After you have taken a few seconds to clarify the question in your own mind, answer it *directly.* Monitor yourself to be sure you stay on the topic, and do not ramble. The interviewer has asked the question because it is important to the job. The questioner is trying to find out about your approach to this particular aspect of the job, not about some related or unrelated topic that comes into your mind. Furthermore, if a point system is used, you will get no points unless you directly answer the question, no matter how insightful and accurate your comments are.

Elaborate—Succinctly

You need to strike a careful balance with your responses. The interview is your chance to give a person who may be a total stranger to you a crash course in who you are and what you can do. Therefore, you need to elaborate on your ideas. The interviewer intends for the questions to produce meaty answers, therefore one-sentence responses are rarely sufficient.

On the other hand, you are in a timed situation, and you do not want to be seen as a motor mouth. If you have taken the rehearsal step seriously, you should be able to explain your ideas fully enough to impress the interviewer without becoming repetitive, tedious, or excruciatingly detailed.

Paint a Picture

One technique that will help you elaborate succinctly is to include concrete examples in your answers. This approach will help you show the interviewer that you not only can discuss theories, philosophies, and teaching approaches but that you have also been successful in applying those ideas.

Examples of Including Specifics in Responses

- I believe that children should be encouraged to take some responsibility for how they behave in the classroom. Therefore, I have students help me come up with classroom procedures and rules the first day. Another way I would promote responsibility is . . .
- I use a workshop approach to writing instruction. To me, this means that students select their own topics and audiences, write at their own paces, and meet with me individually for instruction and feedback. My workshop also includes . . .
- I like to get students actively involved in learning. For example, I had students participate in an ecology program that the county government sponsored. Some of the activities were . . .

Being specific paints a picture of how you operate in a classroom. It lets the interviewer know you are a "can do" person. This approach is an excellent way to let the questioner find out a lot about you in a short period of time.

Do Not Assume

You will be engaging in this conversation so that the interviewer can find out what you know and what you can do. Many interviewees forget this basic fact. This shortcoming is especially true of experienced teachers who are seeking a transfer or promotion. As a result, they do not explain themselves fully. For instance, you might say, "I would be sure that my program is based on state standards." Your line of thinking might be that the interviewer, an elementary supervisor, certainly knows what this means, so you do not have to say any more. The point, however, is that the interviewer wants to see if *you* know what this means and if you define it in a way that is compatible with the district's program, so you *do* need to say more.

Er, Um, When You Do Not Have an Answer

Very likely, the interviewer will ask at least one question for which you are unprepared, no matter how well you have done your homework. In fact, some interviewers ask a question that they think no one will be able to answer just to see how applicants respond to this type of situation. There are a couple of things *not* to do. Do not bluff your way through. Also, do not admit, "Well, I never thought about that . . ." Hearing this response, the interviewer may justifiably think, "Well, why not?"

There are a couple of effective strategies from which you can choose. If you have some thoughts on the subject, honestly say, "I am not sure about that, but my thoughts are . . ." After you have said your thoughts, explain why you think this response is plausible.

Example of a Response to an Unfamiliar Topic

I am not sure how your English as a Second Language program defines preproduction stage, but I think it means a student who responds with nonverbal communication. The reason I think this is because I believe that "preproduction" is equivalent to the stage we called Level 1 in the system where I have been working.

Even if your response is not what the interviewer anticipated, your honesty and your logical thought process in surmising a feasible response will be impressive.

Another route to take, especially if you do not have any idea of the response, it to again admit that you are not sure of the answer and then outline how you would go about finding out. Consider the following example:

Interviewer: We use the Milestones Reading Materials in first grade. What do you know about these and how would you use them with advanced readers?

Possible Response: Being from a school that did not use those materials, I do not have detailed knowledge about them. However, I know that the program consists of leveled big books and small books. I have used big books and little books from the Read On series. Some ways I have used them are . . . I could do several things to find out about Milestones. For instance, I could get some sample materials from the publisher. Also, I could talk with a friend of mine who is a reading specialist and see what she can tell me. Then I could . . .

TONE

As you participate in your interview, remember that it is *your* interview. Letting your unique personality shine through in a professional manner is not only appropriate but also advantageous.

You want to show the interviewer that you are a knowledgeable, experienced, and dedicated professional, and also that you are a likable person. Using some light comments and appropriate humor is fine as long as you keep in mind that, in this setting, the interviewer is not a friend but a potential boss. This may be especially challenging if the interviewer is someone with whom you have worked in the school system or is, in fact, actually a professional or social friend.

Through the tone and content of your responses, let the interviewer see your kind and caring side. Be aware of your interviewer's point of view as well as needs and feelings in the interview situation. While you are stressed about being in the spotlight, the interviewer is concerned about getting the right person for the job, about making you feel as comfortable as possible, and about other commitments and tasks waiting for attention. It is a bonus if you can take some of your attention away from the nervousness you are feeling and help the interviewer feel at ease through a relaxed manner.

BODY LANGUAGE

The importance of eye contact and a firm handshake when you greet the interviewer has already been mentioned. Eye contact continues to be critical throughout the conversation. Looking at the interviewer helps show your confidence and straightforwardness.

For your own ease and to avoid distracting the interviewer's attention, sit in a way that is comfortable and does not necessitate changing positions constantly. Sit with your body facing the interviewer so that eye contact is easy. Lean forward slightly, rather than lounging back in your chair, to let the interviewer know you are fully engaged in the conversation.

Even though it is hard to do when you are in the spotlight, a ready smile will set you both at ease. Of course, a nervous giggle or forced smile could be detrimental. If you are too nervous, especially during the early minutes of the session, to pull off a smile, do not worry. You will loosen up as you go along.

USE OF YOUR PORTFOLIO

Avoid the mistake of waiting until the end of the interview to refer to your portfolio. You have put a lot of work into preparing this document. If you wait until the end, it will probably only get a very cursory glance because the interviewer may feel pressed to get on to the next interview or to another task. You can get more attention for this tool and use it as a resource to help you remember and illustrate points if you have it at your fingertips during the interview. For this reason, it was suggested that you get it out of your briefcase at the beginning and put it on the table in front of you.

Whenever the interviewer asks a question that relates to something in your portfolio, use the tabs to turn to that section. Use the portfolio as a prop in discussing the question at hand. For instance, if you were responding to a question about classroom management, obviously the graphic you created to show how you handle this aspect of teaching would be useful. You could also flip to the page that shows a possible classroom setup and comment briefly on how this plan supports productive behavior by providing accessible materials, workable traffic patterns, and spaces for whole-class and group activities.

In addition to getting use out of the materials you so painstakingly prepared and creating a clearer illustration of you and your teaching style, this ongoing use of your portfolio during the interview will help you be more relaxed. Basically, the portfolio contents will serve as notes to help you remember the thinking you did during your planning stage.

ENDING THE INTERVIEW

If the interviewer has not mentioned it in the course of the conversation, feel free at the end to ask when you can expect to hear something. A principal or supervisor is usually most willing to explain the next steps and how people are contacted about whether they do or do not get the job. Having this information will give you some peace of mind. Also be sure that the interviewer knows how to reach you within the next few days.

When the interviewer signals the end of the conversation, you have a chance to make your final good impression. Smoothly, gather up your materials and put them in your case. A firm handshake with good eye contact and a genuine word of thanks for the chance to meet is a fitting closure.

FINAL THOUGHTS

Interviewing may feel awkward to you, especially if it has been a long time since you have gone through this experience. The spotlight is on you, and the agenda is for you to talk about yourself and to focus on your experiences, accomplishments, and goals. Doing this can be uncomfortable. Doing it in a manner that does not come off as bragging can be challenging.

It can help to think of the interviewer's point of view. A principal or supervisor, in a short period of time, must make an important decision about whom to hire. That decision will have an impact on the school for years to come. There is no time to "date" the candidates and see how they react in various situations. All must be judged based on a few pieces of paper and one or two conversations.

Do whatever you can to allay the interviewer's fears. Find ways to help this person feel confident that you have the experience and dedication to do an outstanding job. Through concrete examples and step-by-step plans, assure the interviewer that you can put into practice educational theory even if that means stepping into a new grade or a new role from the one in which you have been successful in the past. Through your words as well as your demeanor, demonstrate your ability to get along well with others and your willingness to learn new approaches when needed. If you focus on these goals, you will provide responses that make the time you spent preparing fruitful.

CHAPTER ELEVEN

Now What?

The most immediate thing you should consider after an interview is getting together with a supportive friend or family member to celebrate your successful completion of the process. That is right. Even before you know the outcome, give yourself a pat on the back for doing such a thoroughly professional job of preparation and implementation of your plan.

FOLLOW-UP CONTACT

Sending a thank you note to your interviewer as soon as possible after your meeting is a worthwhile idea. This message does not have to be long. It can be on the stationery you have been using for this process or even handwritten on a note card. If you choose the latter, refrain from anything cute. Select a good-quality, plain note card and envelope in a neutral color to reinforce the impression of professionalism.

The purpose of this note is not to convince your interviewer to give you the position. That decision will possibly already be made by the time the note arrives, but this simple courtesy will pave the way for future good relations if you get the job. On the other hand, if another candidate is selected, your note will leave a favorable impression that might help the principal or supervisor think of you if another position for which you are qualified becomes available.

Example of a Follow-Up Letter

May 26, 2004

Dear Dr. James:

I enjoyed meeting with you on May 25. The prospect of becoming an assistant principal at South Elementary is very exciting to me. Your program has a great reputation, and I would like to be part of it.

Our discussion about your interest in starting a mentoring program involving the middle school a block away from South Elementary was especially stimulating. I have been thinking about some of the possibilities and have a lot of ideas about how I might assist with that project. My experience in setting up a tutoring program involving fifth graders and first graders in my current position might provide some ideas.

I look forward to hearing from you. Again, thank you for making time to talk with me.

Sincerely,
Chris Michaels

LETTING GO

Hopefully, the suspense will end quickly, and you will get a phone call within a few days or a week of the interview. If you have not heard anything within the period of time you were told to expect a reply, it is acceptable to wait a few more days and then call to ask the status of the process.

Remember that you may go through the hiring process several times before you are offered and accept a position. Not being offered a particular position does not mean that the person interviewing you thought you were incapable of doing the job. There can be many reasons for a job going to another candidate. For example, perhaps you are well qualified for a transfer you have requested to another school. There may be another candidate, however, who is equally qualified and has been requesting a transfer for a couple of years. If you are applying for an assistant principal position, you may be well qualified, but your strengths and weaknesses may be too similar to the principal's. Maybe the administrator needs someone with complementary skills to provide a balanced program.

In short, if you do not get selected the first time or two, try not to take it personally. Undeniably, going through all the work of preparing for an interview and then not getting the job is difficult, especially if it is one you wanted badly. Remember, however, that most commonly, people interview several times before securing a transfer or new position. Each time you go through the experience, you become more polished and confident. Plus, subsequent interviews will not take as long to prepare as did the first. You can continue using the tools you have already created, such as your résumé and portfolio, either as they are or with slight modifications. Just keep trying. Your time will come.

If you have gone through several interviews and not yet found the position that you are seeking, consider a brave but helpful step. Think about calling one or more of your interviewers and asking for some feedback. Do this in a way that does not put the person on the spot. A "Why didn't I get the transfer?" approach might be off-putting. There are, however, questions that can be helpful. If necessary, remind the person of who you are and the interview you had, then ask a question such as,

- What are some additional things I can do to help prepare for a position in your department (school)?
- Do you have any suggestions of positions that might be a good match for my skills?

If you have tried repeatedly to move to a particular subject, grade, or school with no luck, you should consider putting your energies into another location. It may be that the school where you thought you wanted to transfer is not a good match for your goals, philosophies, and approaches. Putting in a request to go to a different school could result in your being more successful.

WHEN YOU GET THE JOB

Once you get the phone call that you have dreamed of, you will impress your employer by making contact at once to express appreciation for being selected. Find out how you can get any needed materials right away so that you can start planning. Suggest a chance to meet with your new employer so that you can find out about specific expectations and procedures.

This meeting is an important step even if you are transferring to a new grade or role within a school where you have been teaching for years. While you may be thoroughly familiar with the principal's or supervisor's views concerning the grade or subject you have been teaching, that person may have a very different vision of how to handle the position into which you are moving. Your administrator may even be relying on you, as an experienced teacher, to lead your grade level or subject colleagues in a new direction.

When you meet with your supervisor and principal, discipline yourself to spend a significant amount of the time you are with them simply *listening*. Once you start working in the position, you may not have the luxury of a block of time to discuss philosophy and goals. Use the meeting wisely to find out how that person sees your job. Take lots of notes, and be sure to get your most important questions answered. Check out your understanding of what you are being told. For example, if your principal says, "When you become our media specialist, I want you to work with small groups," you might need to clarify, "Do you see me working with *just* small groups or will I also do some whole-class lessons?"

If you have been working in the school and are now moving into a new role, such as reading specialist, it will be important to discuss with your administrator ideas for handling the change in your relationship with other teachers.

FINAL THOUGHTS AND BEST WISHES

This book has set forth a detailed procedure for planning and implementing the process of making a transfer or role change in your career. Certainly, undertaking this process is a lot of work, but if you take on the challenge, your chance of being successful in securing the next step in your professional goals is excellent. So get started on your adventure, and best wishes with the process and your new position.

Index

**CORWIN
PRESS**

The Corwin Press logo—a raven striding across an open book—represents the union of courage and learning. Corwin Press is committed to improving education for all learners by publishing books and other professional development resources for those serving the field of K–12 education. By providing practical, hands-on materials, Corwin Press continues to carry out the promise of its motto: **"Helping Educators Do Their Work Better."**